OCR GCSE

History A
Schools History Project

Elizabethan England

Colette Roberts

www.heinemann.co.uk

✓ Free online support
✓ Useful weblinks
✓ 24 hour online ordering

01865 888080

Official Publisher Partnership

OCR AND HEINEMANN ARE WORKING TOGETHER TO PROVIDE BETTER SUPPORT FOR YOU

Heinemann is an imprint of Pearson Education Limited, a company incorporated in England and Wales, having its registered office at Edinburgh Gate, Harlow, Essex, CM20 2JE. Registered company number: 872828

www.heinemann.co.uk

Heinemann is a registered trademark of Pearson Education Limited

Text © Pearson Education Limited 2009

First published 2009

13 12 11 10 09
10 9 8 7 6 5 4 3 2 1

British Library Cataloguing in Publication Data
A catalogue record for this book is available from the British Library
ISBN 978 0 435501 464

Copyright notice
All rights reserved. No part of this publication may be reproduced in any form or by any means (including photocopying or storing it in any medium by electronic means and whether or not transiently or incidentally to some other use of this publication) without the written permission of the copyright owner, except in accordance with the provisions of the Copyright, Designs and Patents Act 1988 or under the terms of a licence issued by the Copyright Licensing Agency, Saffron House, 6–10 Kirby Street, London EC1N 8TS (www.cla.co.uk). Applications for the copyright owner's written permission should be addressed to the publisher.

Edited by Kim Vernon
Designed by Pearson Education Limited
Typeset by Wearset Ltd, Boldon, Tyne and Wear
Produced by Wearset Ltd, Boldon, Tyne and Wear
Original illustrations © Pearson Education Limited 2009
Illustrated by Wearset Ltd, Boldon, Tyne and Wear
Cover design by Pearson Education Limited
Picture research by Q2AMedia
Cover photo/illustration © iStockPhoto.com/Kasia Biel
Printed and bound in the UK by Scotprint

Acknowledgements
The author and publisher would like to thank the following individuals and organisations for permission to reproduce copyright material:

Page 7 Source G From: *Monarchy and Matrimony*, S. Doran, © 1996 Taylor & Francis. Reproduced by permission of Taylor & Francis Books UK. **Page 40 Source B** From: *Elizabeth I and Religion*, S. Doran, © 1994 Taylor & Francis. Reproduced by permission of Taylor & Francis Books UK. **Page 54 Source B** From: *The Reign of Elizabeth*, S. Lee, © 2007 Taylor & Francis. Reproduced by permission of Taylor & Francis Books UK. **Page 60 Source C** From: *The Reign of Elizabeth*, S. Lee, © 2007 Taylor & Francis. Reproduced by permission of Taylor & Francis Books UK. **Page 77 Source C** Jeff Howell, Associate Professor of History, East Georgia College, Statesboro, Georgia.

From: *Drake, Sir Francis: 'El Draque' The Dragon*. The Historical Text Archive. **Page 77 Source D** The Drake Exploration Society. **Page 77 Source E** The Drake Exploration Society. **Page 77 Source F** The Drake Exploration Society. **Page 83 Source B** J. Fuller, *Decisive Battles of the Western World*, 1954. Orion Books. **Page 83 Source D** From: *England 1485–1603*, HarperCollins Publishers Ltd © 2005 D. Murphy. **Page 85 Source D** From: *The Reign of Elizabeth*, S. Lee, © 2007 Taylor & Francis. Reproduced by permission of Taylor & Francis Books UK.

The author and publisher would like to thank the following individuals and organisations for permission to reproduce photographs:

Page 6 Mary Evans Picture Library. **Page 8** National Museum Wales/The Bridgeman Art Library. **Page 11** George (1684–1756)/Private Collection/The Bridgeman Art Library. **Page 12** Private Collection/Ken Welsh/The Bridgeman Art Library. **Page 14** English School, (16th century)/National Portrait Gallery, London, UK/The Bridgeman Art Library. **Page 15L** Peake, Robert (fl.1580–1626) (attr. to)/Private Collection/The Bridgeman Art Library. **Page 15R** National Portrait Gallery, London. **Page 16L** Zuccari, or Zuccaro, Federico (1540–1609)/Pinacoteca Nazionale, Siena, Italy/Alinari/The Bridgeman Art Library. **Page 16R** Bettmann/Corbis. **Page 19** Nikreates/Alamy. **Page 20** Photolibrary. **Page 22** Cockson, Thomas (fl.1591–1636)/Private Collection/The Stapleton Collection/The Bridgeman Art Library. **Page 24** Interfoto/Mary Evans. **Page 28B** Hulton Archive/Stringer/Getty Images. **Page 28T** Zuccari, or Zuccaro, Federico (1540–1609)/Pinacoteca Nazionale, Siena, Italy/Alinari/The Bridgeman Art Library. **Page 29B** Mary Evans Picture Library. **Page 29M** Mary Evans Picture Library. **Page 29T** Mary Evans Picture Library. **Page 30** Private Collection/The Bridgeman Art Library. **Page 36** Mary Evans Picture Library. **Page 37** The British Library/Photolibrary. **Page 38** Hulsen, Friedrich van (c.1580–1660) Private Collection/The Bridgeman Art Library. **Page 39** Hulton Archive/Getty Images. **Page 41** Topfoto. **Page 48** Beggars and Begging (woodcut) (b/w photo), English School, (16th century)/Private Collection/The Bridgeman Art Library. **Page 51** Cheryl Rowley/Istockphoto. **Page 52** Yorkshire & Humber Grid For Learing. **Page 56** English School, (16th century)/Private Collection/The Bridgeman Art Library. **Page 61** Fotomas/Bridgeman Art Library. **Page 62** Mary Evans Picture Library. **Page 63B** Cheryl Rowley/Istockphoto. **Page 63T** Robin Smith/Photolibrary. **Page 67** Sammlung Rauch/INTERFOTO. **Page 71** Library of Congress. **Page 73** Library of Congress. **Page 74** Library of Congress. **Page 76** National Maritime Museum. **Page 78** English School/The Bridgeman Art Library/Getty Images. **Page 79** Pearson Education Ltd. Debbie Rowe. **Page 82** The Pepys Library, Magdalene College, Cambridge. **Page 83** Timothy Millett Collection/The Bridgeman Art Library. **Page 84** The Bridgeman Art Library/Photolibrary. **Page 85** Mary Evans Picture Library.

Every effort has been made to contact copyright holders of material reproduced in this book. Any omissions will be rectified in subsequent printings if notice is given to the publishers.

Contents

Get ready for your Study in Depth: Elizabethan England

The reign of Elizabeth I has often been referred to as a 'golden age'. She ruled for 45 years. The achievements she is most well known for are the Spanish Armada and the development of literary culture. Less well known are her religious settlements and her manipulation of her public image to win the loyalty of her people.

Modern interpretations of her reign vary from a 'queen among princes' to someone who merely completed the Reformation started by her father. What cannot be denied is that the study of Elizabethan England has fascinated thousands for generations, as shown by the sheer number of books, plays and films produced about her reign.

How this book can help

This book is designed to prepare you in three ways for your Depth Study of Elizabethan England:

1   It provides you with a fascinating insight into this period in history and invites you to explore further.

2   It provides you with all the important information that you will need in order to answer the questions you will face in the exam. It also gives you case studies, which you can use as examples in your answers.

3   It explains the different types of questions you have to answer AND gives you tips and practice to help you improve your performance so that you can reach the highest levels.

What style is the book?

The book is written to stimulate your interest. There are many original sources, a variety of different learning tasks for you to complete, opportunities for you to voice your opinion and to do some historical detective work.

How will the book help me get a better grade?

Throughout the book, the tasks that you are set build up a bank of knowledge about this period. The set tasks help you to develop the skills needed to answer the examination questions. Sample mark schemes are used throughout. These give you a good idea of how long you should spend on the questions, how much you should write, and how many points you should make.

Three essential exam skills

One common misunderstanding among students taking GCSE History is that you need to know massive amounts of detailed information, dates, facts, and so on. This is NOT true! Remember – examiners don't award levels according to how much you write! Candidates who carefully read the questions, and therefore focus on what they are being asked to do, will often reach the top levels WITHOUT writing as much as candidates who misread the questions and/or just write down everything they know. Quality and relevance are what matter, not quantity. For instance, if asked to give reasons why something happened, if you explain several reasons – with a few precise and relevant bits of your own knowledge for each one – you will score much more highly than a candidate who simply writes pages of accurate facts, which just describe what happened.

To do well in GCSE History, you will need a combination of these three skills:

1   Sufficient knowledge to show the examiner that you have followed a course (and paid attention!) AND done some serious revision.

2   The ability to USE the information you've remembered to answer the different types of questions you will be asked – such as those that ask you to EXPLAIN something.

3   The ability to understand sources and explain what they do and do not tell us about a particular event or topic; how they are and are not useful; why they might have different views or attitudes; and how to add your own knowledge to what is and is not given by the source or sources.

This book will help you with all three of these skills and abilities, providing you with the necessary knowledge AND giving you practice with typical questions to improve your exam technique. Every year, examiners mark papers of History students who show good knowledge but fail to use it effectively when answering the questions.

GradeStudio

Helping you to write better answers

Throughout each chapter, you will find Grade Studio activities, which include practice questions to help you develop the skills necessary to answer different types of questions in the exam. Each Grade Studio activity is accompanied by Examiner's Tips. In the Grade Studio section at the end of each chapter, you will find an exam-style question. This explains the mark schemes the examiners apply to each type of question, and then gives you a typical sample answer with examiner's comments that include precise tips and advice on how the candidate could have pushed their answer into the top levels. You will then have the chance to produce your own (better!) answer.

By the time you have worked your way through this book, you will have had plenty of practice at all the different types of questions you will meet – and plenty of tips and advice to make sure that when you meet them in the exam, you will know exactly how to answer them in ways that will get you full marks.

Top revision tips

The final part of preparing yourself for this exam is, of course, revision. This can be boring, especially if all you do is reread or rewrite your textbooks and notes several times. However, variety does make it seem less so – and actually has positive benefits in terms of helping the brain to learn the necessary facts AND skills. While everyone has different methods to suit them best, the following are a few general tips, which should benefit everyone.

1. Make a revision plan. List the topics you have to learn and spread them across your revision timetable. Do not leave the ones you struggle with or dislike until the last. Equal time has to be given to each topic.

2. Work in 40-minute blocks, then have a break for 10 minutes. When you have finished your revision for the evening, spend at least 10 minutes recapping or being tested on your learning.

3. Keep your brain well supplied with water and food – especially when you're thinking. Your brain will need at least 70 per cent of all the energy your body takes in if it is to function well.

4. Use a variety of revision techniques. This will stop you getting bored but will also tap into your different styles of learning – visual, audio and kinaesthetic.

5. Work with a conscientious friend, and test each other on the various topics. They may be able to provide you with help on topics you find difficult and vice versa. You can also exchange ideas for how best to remember bits of knowledge and skills.

Good luck!

Chapter 1

Was Elizabeth I Gloriana?

Before 1558

On the death of her father, Henry VIII, Elizabeth I's brother, Edward VI, ascended the throne. He was only nine years old and so was advised by regents, first by the Duke of Somerset and then by the Duke of Northumberland. The reign featured religious changes, poor trade and bad harvests. It also featured rebellions. On his premature death in 1553, Edward VI's sister Mary I became queen. She restored the Catholic religion and persecuted anyone who continued to follow the Protestant religion by burning them at the stake. Mary I's popularity with the people of England was further damaged by her marriage to the King of Spain. Again, rebellions featured heavily, as did public executions of the ringleaders. This period has become known as the mid-Tudor crisis. It was into this troubled situation that Elizabeth I ascended the throne in 1558.

Holiness

Temperance

Chastity

Friendship

Justice

Courtesy

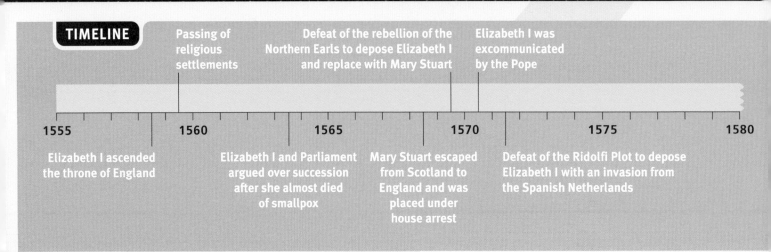

TIMELINE

Passing of religious settlements

Defeat of the rebellion of the Northern Earls to depose Elizabeth I and replace with Mary Stuart

Elizabeth I was excommunicated by the Pope

1555 — 1560 — 1565 — 1570 — 1575 — 1580

Elizabeth I ascended the throne of England

Elizabeth I and Parliament argued over succession after she almost died of smallpox

Mary Stuart escaped from Scotland to England and was placed under house arrest

Defeat of the Ridolfi Plot to depose Elizabeth I with an invasion from the Spanish Netherlands

Only two years after Elizabeth I's death, Catholics plotted to kill the king, James I, and his Parliament in the Gunpowder Plot. Thirty-seven years after Elizabeth I's death, Parliament tried to reduce the power of the monarch and a civil war began. Unlike Elizabeth I, the kings that followed were unable to manipulate the power of their leading nobles. Increase upon increase in taxation did little to encourage the common people to stay loyal to their king. In 1600, Elizabeth was portrayed as Gloriana in an epic poem by Edmund Spenser called *The Faerie Queene*. Gloriana (The Faerie Queene herself) represented all that was good: chastity, holiness and justice. But some historians have claimed that the problems future monarchs had were the true legacy of Elizabeth I. They point out that her failure to deal with issues such as the succession and the sale of crown lands to finance war may illustrate her disregard for the future.

ACTIVITY

Imagine you have lived through the 'mid-Tudor crisis' and Elizabeth I has just come to the throne. You are a London merchant and you are looking at this portrait of the new queen.

- What are your first impressions?
- How might you describe the queen to your wife when you get home? Would your account be positive towards the queen or negative?
- Read the words at the side of the portrait. Write them in the order you think is most important to you for a successful monarch.
- Rewrite them in the order you think Elizabeth I might think is most important. Are there any differences?

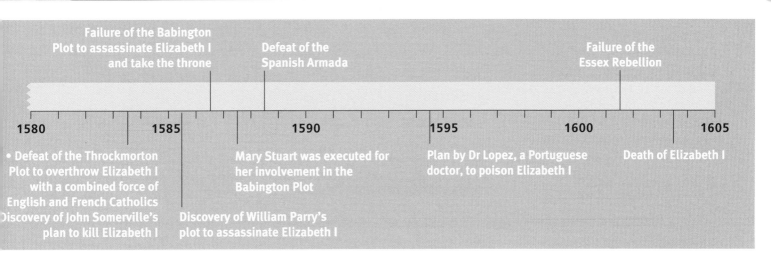

Failure of the Babington Plot to assassinate Elizabeth I and take the throne

Defeat of the Spanish Armada

Failure of the Essex Rebellion

1580   1585   1590   1595   1600   1605

• Defeat of the Throckmorton Plot to overthrow Elizabeth I with a combined force of English and French Catholics
Discovery of John Somerville's plan to kill Elizabeth I

Discovery of William Parry's plot to assassinate Elizabeth I

Mary Stuart was executed for her involvement in the Babington Plot

Plan by Dr Lopez, a Portuguese doctor, to poison Elizabeth I

Death of Elizabeth I

1.1 How difficult was the situation on Elizabeth I's accession?

LEARNING OBJECTIVES

In this lesson you will:
- learn about the immediate difficulties facing Elizabeth I
- practise using source comprehension skills.

KEY WORDS

Accession – *taking up the position of king or queen.*

Allies – *friends or countries who are joined for a common reason, usually to protect and defend each other and particularly in times when there is a threat of war.*

Stereotypes – *deeply entrenched ideas.*

Elizabeth I's immediate problems

Elizabeth I faced multiple problems on her **accession**. These arose from difficult political and religious situations and each problem demanded her immediate attention.

The political problems she faced arose from relationships England had with foreign countries, the increasing economic crisis in England and because of her gender. Not only did Elizabeth I have to deal with **stereotypical** ideas of the role and limitations of women, but this was made worse by the past actions and inactions of the latter years of her sister Mary I's reign.

Foreign affairs demanded her attention. Her reign began with England at war with France and **allied** to Spain. It ended with England at war with Spain and allied to France. There were also political problems closer to home. Scotland was causing serious difficulties on the northern border of England.

All of this wartime activity affected patterns of trade and put a huge taxation burden on the English people. A rapid rise in population and poor harvests considerably reduced the number of jobs available and the level of wages being paid at a time when food prices were at their highest (see Source A).

It was certainly a very challenging start to her reign.

SOURCE

Year	Foodstuffs	Industrial products
1491–1500	100	97
1501–10	106	98
1511–20	116	102
1521–30	159	110
1531–40	161	110
1541–50	217	127
1551–60	315	186
1561–70	298	218
1571–80	341	223
1581–90	389	230
1591–1600	530	238
1601–10	527	256

Index of prices 1491–1610.

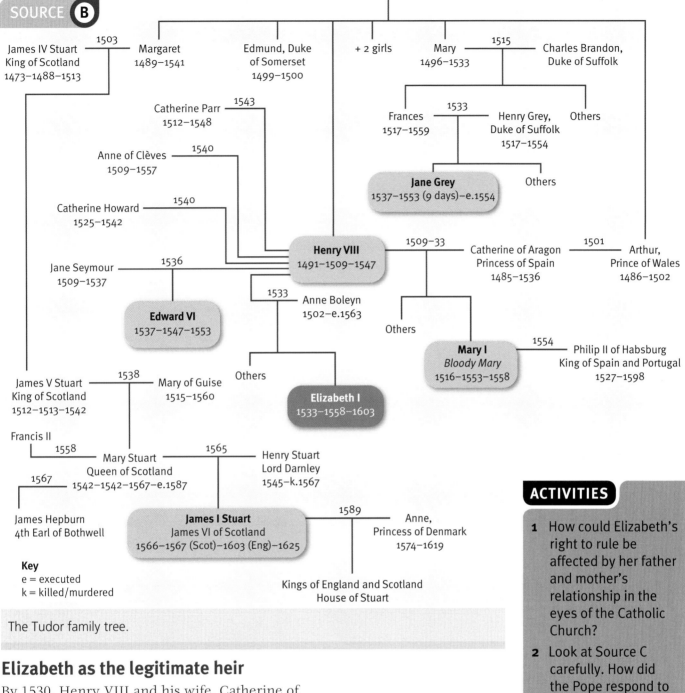

The Tudor family tree.

Key
e = executed
k = killed/murdered

Elizabeth as the legitimate heir

By 1530, Henry VIII and his wife, Catherine of Aragon, had only one child, a daughter called Mary (see Source B). Henry VIII firmly believed that a son was vital to lead the country on his death. Catherine was too old to have more children and so Henry VIII had turned his attentions to one of her ladies in waiting, Anne Boleyn. When Henry VIII discovered that Anne was pregnant, he was desperate to marry her before the child was born illegitimate, in case it was a son. The Catholic Church and the Pope would not allow the divorce so Henry VIII broke away from the Church in Rome and made himself Supreme Head of the Church in England. He divorced Catherine and married Anne and the child they had was Elizabeth.

ACTIVITIES

1 How could Elizabeth's right to rule be affected by her father and mother's relationship in the eyes of the Catholic Church?

2 Look at Source C carefully. How did the Pope respond to Elizabeth as Queen of England?

SOURCE C

Elizabeth, the pretended Queen of England, has seized the place of the Supreme Head of the Church in England... We do declare her to be deprived of her pretended title. We do command all noblemen and people not to obey her or her orders.

Orders issued by the Pope in 1570.

Elizabeth's religious problems

Henry VIII had to marry a third time before he produced a male heir, Edward. Edward VI became king on his father's death and introduced wholesale changes to make the English national religion Protestant. Due to ill health, he only ruled for a short time, and then his eldest half-sister Mary I took over the throne at his death. Daughter of a Spanish mother (Catherine of Aragon), Mary I was a Catholic and persecuted Protestants, having them burned at the stake in a bid to convert England back to Catholicism. However, Mary I died childless and so Elizabeth, her half-sister, took the throne.

On her accession, Elizabeth I made it clear to her subjects that she would deal with religion with the same enthusiasm and commitment as she would her other royal duties. The country, which had undergone decades of religious turmoil held its breath – which religion would she choose?

SOURCE E

... how dangerous it is to make alteration in religion, especially in the beginning of a prince's reign.

Advice of Armagil Waad to Elizabeth I about hasty action with regard to religion.

ACTIVITY

According to Sources D and E, why did Elizabeth need to take particular care over her religious decisions as she became queen?

SOURCE D

Mary I put to death over 300 Protestants during her reign, gaining her the nickname 'Bloody Mary' after her death.

The rule of a woman

Like Mary before her Elizabeth had problems simply because she was a woman. Throughout her reign Englishmen believed it was contrary to nature for a woman to exercise authority over men, even within a family. Therefore it followed that it was unnatural for a woman to rule the realm. This led to an assumption that Elizabeth would marry. A husband could take over ruling the realm but even more importantly he could produce an heir to the throne. Throughout her reign Parliament petitioned the Queen on this matter, pleading her to marry.

ACTIVITIES

1   According to Source F, what was the general opinion of a woman ruler? Explain why?

2   Look at Source G carefully. How does it suggest Elizabeth would have explained her reasons for not marrying?

3   Look at Source B. If Elizabeth did not produce an heir who would be next in line to the throne? Why would this be a problem for the people of England?

SOURCE F

Thou hast set to rule over us a woman, whom nature hath formed to be into subjection unto man, and whom thou by thine holy apostle commandest to keep silence and not to speak in the congregation. Ah Lord! To take away the empire from a man, and give it to a woman, seemeth to be an evident token of thine anger towards us Englishmen.

Thomas Becon, speaking about Mary I in 1554.

SOURCE G

Some were of the opinion that she was fully resolved in her mind that she might better provide both for the commonwealth and her own glory by an unmarried life than by marriage, as foreseeing that if she married a subject she would disparage herself by the inequality of the match, and give occasion of domestically heartburnings, private grudges and commotions; if stranger she would then subject both herself and her people to a foreign yoke and endanger religion.

Susan Doran, writing about Elizabeth I in *Monarchy and Matrimony*, 1996.

ACTIVITIES

4   Look at all the sources carefully. Use the information on these pages to create an ideas map to show the immediate problems faced by Elizabeth I.

5   When you have finished your ideas map, circle the different effects – political, economic or religious – to weigh up in which area Elizabeth I had the biggest problems. Are there any causes that appear in both categories? This is a frequent area you will be tested on in the examination. Make your own judgement now in preparation.

BRAIN BOOST

Ideas maps are a really effective way to revise. Remember to turn your page to landscape and draw curved arrows to reflect the way that your brain processes information and to aid your memory through your peripheral vision. Use symbols and pictures as well as words to represent the information to tap into all of your visual learning style. Dividing the material in this way will allow you to quickly process the information in order to answer a question that asks you to 'briefly describe the...'

BRAIN BOOST

Begin your ideas map again, without looking at any of the information. Try to visualise what your original map looked like. When you are struggling, look back at it. Continue until the ideas map is complete. This is a very effective form of revision but is also a good way to practise an essay plan for a potential question.

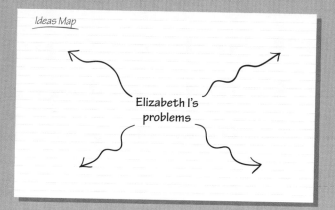

Ideas Map

Elizabeth I's problems

1.2 What were Elizabeth I's aims as monarch?

LEARNING OBJECTIVES

In this lesson you will:

- learn about the aims of Elizabeth I as monarch
- practise cross-referencing sources.

KEY WORDS

Differentiate – *show the differences between things.*

Aims of Elizabeth I

The aims of Elizabeth I's diplomacy were simple. She needed to establish herself as the rightful queen of England, emphasising her royal lineage. She needed to assert her authority and for it to be accepted without question. To do this she had to develop her popularity among her people and their loyalty to her. The more who favoured her as queen, the less likely there would be uprisings. People had to be sure of her abilities as a woman and a Tudor. Elizabeth I knew that she needed to **differentiate** herself from some of the more immediate rulers of the past such as Mary I, her sister, and their over-reliance on Catholicism and foreign alliances. If she could discredit such rulers' actions, it would make her appear to be the better monarch and the saviour of England.

Elizabeth I needed to ensure the safety and security of the kingdom entrusted to her. She had no aims to make political or religious alliances with any foreign country. She aimed instead to use or avoid alliances as and when it was useful to do so.

SOURCE A

The Tudor succession, painted in 1572. King Philip II of Spain and Mary I (to the left of the picture) are accompanied by Mars, the god of war. Elizabeth I (to the right of the picture, without a male partner, is accompanied by the symbols of peace and prosperity. Edward VI kneels by his father.

Analysis of sources

How far do Sources A and B agree about the aims of Elizabeth I in the early years of her reign?   [5 marks]

Follow the steps in the table to the question.

Step 1 Describe what Source A shows	Step 2 Describe what Source B shows	Step 3 Explain how the two sources agree but also how they disagree
Source A shows the Tudor family with Elizabeth accompanied by symbols of peace and prosperity and Mary I accompanied by the god of war. This shows how Elizabeth's aims are different to her sister's. She wants to bring peace and prosperity to England whilst Mary I had only brought war.	Source B shows Elizabeth's new ideas about religion, the respect she would show her people, and how her intelligence and sense of justice would bring peace to her people and end corruption and ignorance.	The two sources agree on the aims of Elizabeth. Source B gives additional aims of promoting the love of her subjects and making the necessary religious changes.

Examiner's tip

On the surface, sources will often appear to agree/disagree. Look deeper than the surface of the source. If you analyse the link between the content of the sources or the tone and attitude they take towards an issue, you may find a way in which they agree or disagree.

SOURCE B

Pure religion did tread upon superstition and ignorance; love of subjects did tread upon rebellion and insolency; wisdom did tread upon folly and vainglory; justice did tread upon adulation and bribery.

The official account of Elizabeth I's coronation procession, as printed to the people.

SOURCE C

To be a king and wear a crown is a thing more glorious to them that see it than it is pleasant to them that bear it. For myself, I was never so much enticed with the glorious name of a king or royal authority of a queen, as delighted that God hath made me His instrument to maintain His truth and glory, and to defend this kingdom from peril, dishonour, tyranny and oppression. There will never a queen sit in my seat with more zeal to my country, care to my subjects, and that will sooner with willingness venture her life for her good and safety, than myself. For it is not my desire to live nor reign longer than my life and reign shall be for your good. And though you have had and may have many princes more mighty and wise sitting in this seat, yet you never had or shall have any that will [be] more careful and loving.

Elizabeth I's speech to Parliament in 1601.

ACTIVITY

Source C gives more aims of the rule of Queen Elizabeth I. How far does it agree with Sources A and B?

1.3 What was Elizabeth I's concept of sovereignty and monarchy?

LEARNING OBJECTIVES

In this lesson you will:
- learn about Elizabeth I's concept of sovereignty
- practise using source comprehension skills.

KEY WORDS

Divine Right of Kings – *the belief that the queen or king had been chosen by God to rule the country and therefore should not be disobeyed.*

Protestant – *a follower of a Christian movement separate from Roman Catholicism and the authority of the Pope.*

Sovereignty – *supremacy as ruler.*

Elizabeth I's idea of queenship

Elizabeth I became queen at the age of 25. She was a well-educated and intelligent woman who had observed and learned quickly during the reign of her father (Henry VIII), her brother (Edward VI) and then her sister (Mary I). As a **Protestant**, Elizabeth I had been a potential figurehead for any plot to overthrow the Catholic Mary I. When Thomas Wyatt led a Protestant rebellion against Mary I, Princess Elizabeth was implicated and put in the Tower of London. From this experience she learned the need to be calculating and careful.

Few people in Tudor England would have dared question the monarch or the **Divine Right of Kings** to rule as chosen by God. Elizabeth I used this to her advantage. She fiercely defended her right as queen to suspend and dissolve Parliament, declare war and make peace, appoint and dismiss ministers, determine her own marriage and name her successor. This was a time before there was a regular full-time army to keep peace or a civil service to keep order through laws. Elizabeth I, therefore, partly relied on the patronage of her nobles to keep order. The total belief in her right to rule is shown in the way she gave orders. Elizabeth I was more feared and obeyed than even her father had been.

SOURCE C

When she received visitors in the Privy Chamber at Whitehall, she would pose in front of the Holbein mural of the Tudor dynasty, under the dominating figure of Henry. Her descent from a King legitimated her rule, her descent from that king enhanced her authority.

C. Haigh, *Elizabeth I*, 1998.

GETTING STARTED

With a partner, discuss the current Queen of England. Who is she? What jobs do the Queen and the royal family do? When and where do you see images of them and hear their speeches? What does the Queen mean to you? Who will rule after the Queen? Why will they rule next? How do you feel about this? Bear all of this discussion in mind when you study Elizabeth I's concept of **sovereignty**.

SOURCE

The burden that is fallen upon me maketh me amazed and yet, considering I am God's creature, ordained to obey His appointment, I will thereunto yield, desiring from the bottom of my heart that I may have assistance of His grace to be the minister of His heavenly will in this office now committed to me.

Elizabeth I, speaking to her council at the beginning of her reign.

SOURCE

I would not maintain or support any subject in disobedience against their prince, for besides how this would offend my own conscience, I know that Almighty God may well punish me with the same trouble in my own realm.

Adapted from Elizabeth I's speech to Parliament, 1565.

The Holbein mural at Whitehall of the Tudor dynasty, which Elizabeth I would pose in front of to give herself gravitas.

ACTIVITIES

1 Read Source A carefully.
   - What evidence is there that Elizabeth I believed in the Divine Right of Kings?
   - How could Elizabeth I have used this widely held belief to her advantage?
2 Source B outlines how Elizabeth I believed that the Divine Right of Kings made her part of a network of princes and kings from all over the world, who were all chosen by God.
   - How did she feel about actions to depose other rulers?
   - Why did she feel this way?
   - How do you think this would have affected her actions against her own cousin, Mary, Queen of Scots, who was named as the figurehead of many plots to overthrow her?
3 Read Source C carefully. What does Haigh mean? Why does he point out Henry VIII particularly as adding authority to Elizabeth I's rule?

VOICE YOUR OPINION!

How legitimate do you feel Elizabeth I's claim to the throne was? Discuss her position with regard to her gender, her religion and her parentage.

Recently, the government has discussed whether it is time to change the ancient right of the throne passing to male heirs before their female relations. Do you think this concept is out of date? What arguments could you put forward in favour and against changing this ancient tradition? Make sure that you include information about Elizabeth I as an example to illustrate both sides of the argument.

1.4 What were the strengths and weaknesses of Elizabeth I as a monarch?

LEARNING OBJECTIVES

In this lesson you will:

- understand the strengths and weaknesses of Elizabeth I as a monarch
- make a balanced historical judgement.

KEY WORDS

Irresolution – *lack of decision or purpose.*
Self-interest – *main concern is the promotion of oneself.*

GETTING STARTED

Think about the different strengths that you need to lead a team of people. Make a list of what you think are the ten most important strengths. Can you think of a leader who possesses all of these features? What weaknesses do they have? How do they overcome these weaknesses? Is it okay for a leader to have weaknesses?

Strengths and weaknesses of Elizabeth I

During the Tudor period, Elizabeth I was held up as a celebrated ruler. She dominated the era so much that her reign became known as the 'Elizabethan age'. Her reputation stands very high among later English monarchs. Her wit, intellect, beauty and resolve became known around the world. More recently, historians such as Christopher Haigh have pointed out flaws in her character and the way that she ruled. He portrays her as often difficult and by her constant interference, made problems worse.

Prone to sudden changes of mind

'Elizabeth I The Rainbow Portrait' by Isaac Oliver, 1600.
Elizabeth holds a rainbow in her right hand which symbolises peace. The serpent on her left sleeve represents wisdom, the flowers on her dress symbolise virginity and the eyes and ears on her cloak imply that she sees and hears all.

Sometimes indecisive, delaying key decisions

Deeply religious and very moral

Able to disconnect her personal feelings

Intellectual and very analytical

Dominant and distrustful of others

A skilful propagandist

Thrifty   Self-controlled

Able to chastise anyone

Found it hard to delegate

An excellent speaker

Disliked **self-interest**

Cautious and calculating

Anxious with much nervous energy

Irritable, bad tempered and sometimes violent

Frequently involved in minor issues

Jealous of others

Total self-confidence

Queen Elizabeth… Owing to her courage and to her great power of mind… Declines to rely on anyone save herself, although she is most gracious to all.

Michael Soriano, Spanish Ambassador in 1561.

I would to God her Majesty could be content to refer these things to them that can best judge of them as other princes do.

Francis Walsingham to William Cecil about Elizabeth I.

*This **irresolution** doth weary and kill her ministers, destroy her actions and overcome all good designs and counsels.*

Thomas Smith in 1575.

She is much attached to her people and is very sure that they love her, which is indeed true. She seems to me very much more feared than her sister, and gives her orders and has her way as completely as her father did.

The Spanish Ambassador to England, writing to King Philip II of Spain in 1559.

The constitution of her mind is exempt from female weakness, and she is endowed with masculine power of application. No apprehension can be quicker than hers, no memory more retentive. French and Italian she speaks like English, Latin, with fluency, propriety and judgment; she also spoke Greek with me, frequently, willingly and moderately well …

Robert Ascham Elizabeth's tutor, speaking to a friend about her when Elizabeth was 16 years old.

The Queen stamps with her feet at ill news and thrusts her rusty sword at times into the arras [a tapestry screen] in great rage.

John Harrington, Elizabeth's godson, October 1602.

ACTIVITIES

1. Look at the painting of Elizabeth I on page 12 and the scattered words and phrases. List which words and phrases you think suggest strengths, which you think suggest weaknesses and which you think suggest both. Explain your choice in each case.

2. Read each source carefully. Copy and complete the following table.

   In column 2 of the table, identify which of Elizabeth's strengths and which of her weaknesses would have led people to say the things they said about her.

   In column 3, explain how each strength or weakness would have enabled people to draw these conclusions about her.

3. Did Elizabeth I possess the right qualities to be Queen of England?

Source	Strength/weaknesses that would have led to people speaking about Elizabeth I in this way	How each strength/weakness would have enabled people to draw these conclusions
A		
B		
C		
D		
E		
F		

1.5 Was Elizabeth I successful in winning the loyalty of her people?

LEARNING OBJECTIVES

In this lesson you will:
- learn about how successful Elizabeth I was in winning the loyalty of her people
- practise cross-referencing and assessing the usefulness of sources.

KEY WORDS

Loyalty – *a feeling of duty and devotion towards someone.*

Progresses – *very public royal tours where the queen would travel to different parts of the country, greeting her people.*

What methods did Elizabeth I use to win the loyalty of her people?

Elizabeth I is generally seen as one of the most popular monarchs in English history. She was very much the 'people's queen'. This, however, was not by chance. Elizabeth I held carefully planned parades, particularly in London on significant dates, such as Accession Day. These were lavish displays to remind her subjects of their **loyalty** to her.

On 14 January 1559, on the eve of Coronation Day itself, Elizabeth I took part in a coronation procession through London. It was evident even at this early stage that Queen Elizabeth was signalling the dawn of a golden age. The parade incorporated orations and pageants and she made sure all that attended were 'wonderfully ravished'. So much so, that the next day when she was presented for the people's acceptance, the crowds roared with appreciation.

Royal progresses

At a time when travelling across country was very difficult due to the poor condition of the roads, achieving such parades outside London was more challenging. However, almost every year throughout her reign, Elizabeth I and her court packed up and went on ten week summer **progresses**. They would spend the summer at the houses of the richest nobles in the land. However, not one to miss an opportunity, Elizabeth would travel on a carefully staged route passing as many towns and villages as possible on the way. Before travelling she would find out as much as possible about the area she would be passing through so that she could talk knowledgeably to the people she met and be aware of the problems they might have. Along the way she would also give out alms.

SOURCE A

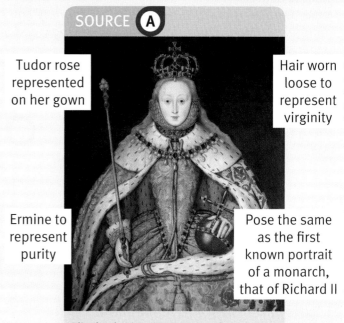

Tudor rose represented on her gown

Hair worn loose to represent virginity

Ermine to represent purity

Pose the same as the first known portrait of a monarch, that of Richard II

Elizabeth I in coronation robes.

ACTIVITIES

1 How did Elizabeth I use her coronation ceremony and the official portraits of it to her advantage so early in her reign? (See Source A.)
2 What ideas about sovereignty was she trying to reinforce?

Although the areas she visited were never north of Stafford or west of Bristol, each progress was given wide publicity for maximum impact. Elizabeth wanted to present herself as the mother, wife, sister and godmother of the people. She knew that loyal subjects would more readily accept bad harvests, slumps in trade, expensive foreign wars, rising prices and unsettled religious changes.

Painted in 1600, this portrait of Elizabeth I and her royal courtiers shows her popularity and loyalty among her royal court. Elizabeth I attempted to control her richest, most powerful noblemen by drawing them into personal, emotional and political relationships with her. Their loyalty was rewarded with positions of power, royal favour and tax concessions.

Images of Elizabeth

Contemporary portraits painted of Elizabeth were symbolic rather than true representations. This was intentional: in 1563 a proclamation was drafted forbidding any further pictures of the queen to be painted until a master version had been created that all others should copy. Although it was never made law, from 1575 all portraits were based on the Darnley portrait (see Source C). In 1594 the decision was taken for artists to only paint pictures which showed the queen as eternally youthful to prevent fears for the future as no successor had been declared. Two years later, in 1596, the Privy Council went as far as ordering all unseemly portraits to be destroyed.

ACTIVITIES

5 How useful is Source D for historians in assessing Elizabeth I's success in winning the loyalty of her people? Think about:
- the speaker
- the audience
- the use of propaganda to convince people they were part of something special.

6 In order to win the loyalty of her people, Elizabeth I presented herself as a 'loving queen'. How far do Sources D and E agree about her image as a 'loving queen' and her success at securing their loyalty using this strategy? Think about:
- what the sources agree upon
- what the sources do not agree upon
- why their interpretations may differ – look at the attribution of the source.

Elizabeth I by an unknown artist, 1575.

ACTIVITIES

3 Look at Source B. Describe the impact of progresses on rich and poor alike.

4 Look at Source C carefully. Why would this portrait have been chosen as the portrait other artists should copy?

Your love for me is of such a kind as has never been known or heard of in the memory of man. Love of this nature is not possessed by parents, it happens not among friends, no, not even among lovers, whose fortune does not always include fidelity, as experience teaches. It is such love as neither persuasion, nor threats nor curses can destroy. Time has no power over it. Time, which eats away iron and wears away the rocks, cannot sever this love of yours. It is of your services consist, and they are of such kind that I would think they would be eternal, if only I were to be eternal.

Elizabeth I, speaking to Oxford students in 1592.

The Queen is but a woman, and ruled by noblemen, and the noblemen and gentlemen are all but one and the gentlemen and farmers will hold together so that the poor can get nothing... we shall never have a merry world while the Queen liveth.

An Essex labourer speaking in 1591.

TAKING IT FURTHER

Find out more about the loyalty of those at Elizabeth I's court. Find out if they really were loyal to the Queen or if they had alternative motives. Christopher Hatton joined the Royal Court in 1564. How did he become a royal favourite? What benefits did he get from becoming close to Elizabeth I?

1.6 How far did Elizabeth I's image reflect reality?

LEARNING OBJECTIVES

In this lesson you will:
- understand how far Elizabeth I's image reflected reality
- draw a balanced conclusion.

KEY WORDS

Line of succession – *in line to the throne of England.*

Privy Council – *the committee that advises the queen.*

What was the true image of Elizabeth?

So good at playing the role of queen, as shown in the royal progresses and processions, there is actually very little evidence of the real person behind the public image. Was Elizabeth really a vulnerable, frightened, lonely person behind the façade, or was she the powerful, confident person that is portrayed in the many contemporary paintings of her? And were all the attributes she was so keen to publicise in her portraits, such as purity and the desire to bring peace and prosperity to England, really true?

Source A shows Elizabeth in sombre dress and holding a sieve which is a symbol of chastity and purity. Other symbolic references are the globe showing England's conquest of the New World and in the background to the left are 'roundels' with images taken from the story of Aeneas and Dido which may be a reference to Elizabeth's rejection of marriage (like Aeneas) in a desire to rule a powerful nation.

Source B shows another very powerful image of the Queen. Here she wears jewel encrusted robes showing her wealth. Beside her is the sword of state symbolising justice, she holds in her right hand an olive branch symbolising peace and the ermine on her left arm represents purity.

SOURCE **A**

'The Sieve Portrait' by Quentin Metsys the Younger (c.1580–1583).

SOURCE **B**

'The Ermine Portrait' by Nicholas Hilliard, 1585.

1590s... war, military recruitment, heavy taxation, harvest failure, trade disruption and unemployment combined to create economic and social crisis. The living standards of wage earners fell to their lowest for 250 years. In 1595–96 there were widespread riots against high food prices. In despair the poor resorted to theft, their superiors resorted to the gallows.

C. Haigh, a modern historian, in *Elizabeth I*, 1998, p. 165.

However, as Source C suggests, Elizabeth's reign was not a time of prosperity and peace as Elizabeth wished to portray in her portraits. Her claim to be the virgin queen is also thought to be in doubt. It was a widely held belief that she was the mistress of Robert Dudley, whom she promoted to important positions within her court. It was even rumoured that she was carrying his child. When Dudley's wife died after falling in mysterious circumstances down the stairs, it was alleged that she had been poisoned so that Dudley would be free to marry Elizabeth. Elizabeth did nothing to suppress these rumours but exacerbated them by spending an excessive amount of time with Dudley. It also came to light that she and Dudley had made arrangements with the Spanish Catholics to make concessions on religion in England if they supported a marriage between them.

Was Elizabeth I's image as an adored queen a reality?

Elizabeth portrayed an image of herself to her subjects and those abroad as a popular queen loved by her people. The number of plots to depose her throughout her reign tend to suggest that in reality this was not so. Source D also suggests that Elizabeth was unable to trust anybody even though they showed the pretence of love towards her. Perhaps the true portrait of Elizabeth is the one of a frightened and lonely woman!

In 1584, Elizabeth I's **Privy Council** felt it necessary to produce the Bond of Association which was signed by hundreds of noblemen. It stated that anyone plotting against the queen in the line of succession, even if they were unaware of the plot, would be excluded from the **line of succession** and executed. The following year Parliament passed the Act of Accession which stated that anyone benefiting from the death of the Queen would be executed.

I have to deal with nobles of divers humours, and peoples who, although they make great demonstration of love towards me, nevertheless were fickle and inconstant, and I have to fear everything.

Elizabeth I in 1597, writing to the French Ambassador.

GradeStudio

Recall and select knowledge

1 a Copy the table and using your knowledge, complete column 2 to explain how Elizabeth I manipulated her image.

b Complete column 3 using the information in this spread.

2 Using the information in the table answer the following question:
How far did Elizabeth's image reflect reality?

Elizabeth I's image	How Elizabeth I manipulated her image	In what ways this image might not have reflected reality
The 'virgin queen'		
Popular queen loved by all her subjects		
Loving 'mother' who cared for all her subjects		
Figure-head providing peace and prosperity to the land		
Others		

Examiner's tip

Make sure that you outline what Elizabeth I's image was, which parts of that image reflected the truth and which parts did not. Remember to conclude with your own judgement.

1.7 Get your sources sorted!

What threat did Mary, Queen of Scots, pose to Elizabeth I?

LEARNING OBJECTIVES

In this lesson you will:

- understand the threat to Elizabeth I posed by Mary, Queen of Scots
- practise answering cross-referencing of sources questions.

KEY WORDS

Attribution – *the writing, usually underneath the source, that describes who it was produced by, when, who the audience were, and sometimes why it was produced.*

Inference – *something that is suggested.*

Mary, Queen of Scots and the question of succession

As the Catholic Queen of Scotland, Mary Stuart, Elizabeth's cousin, already posed a threat to Protestant England. However, Mary was also married to Francis II of France, another Catholic country. Elizabeth I feared this union could lead to a Catholic invasion of England through its northern borders. Only two years after Mary's marriage, Francis II died and Mary was forced to return to Scotland where she married Henry Darnley, bearing a son, James. In a time when Elizabeth I refused to marry, produce an heir or name a successor, Elizabeth was very aware that Mary Stuart might be considered by some to be a better choice for the position of Queen of England.

The situation worsened. Mary's husband, Darnley, was mysteriously killed and she was married to the Earl of Bothwell. Mary was implicated in the death of Darnley and lost support from both Catholic and Protestant Scottish nobles. Imprisoned, she was forced to resign the crown and her son James was crowned King of Scotland.

In 1568 Mary fled Scotland to England. What was Elizabeth I to do with her?

Why was Mary such a difficult problem for Elizabeth?

Elizabeth had various options as to what to do with Mary. She could send her back to Scotland but Elizabeth knew she would be enabling people in Scotland to punish Mary which was against the principle of the Divine Right of Kings which claimed that kings and queens were only answerable to God so it was sinful for subjects to judge or resist them. Also Mary never abandoned hope of returning to Scotland and eventually succeeding Elizabeth as Queen of England. Another option was to welcome Mary at court but Elizabeth knew that if Mary became too popular she would be one step closer to taking the throne. Mary was beautiful and a threat to Elizabeth's popularity in court. The third option was to keep Mary prisoner but with full honour as a queen. This was what Elizabeth did.

Whilst Mary was imprisoned, Elizabeth was repeatedly pressed by Parliament and her Privy Council to have Mary executed, but Elizabeth refused to let this happen. Mary would have continued to reside in prison if it hadn't have been for the impatience of her Catholic supporters who were keen to depose Elizabeth and crown Mary as Queen of England.

What is a 'cross-referencing of sources' question?

In your GCSE examination, you will be tested on your ability to cross-reference sources. This is a high-level historical skill requiring you to combine your source comprehension skills with your ability to compare and contrast, highlighting similarities

SOURCE Ⓐ

She had the ability of winning men's loyalties despite the most outrageous and most foolish deeds. Of her famous beauty her surviving portraits provide little evidence. She was passionate, intelligent, given to violent moods of joy and depression, and entirely without common sense.

A historian's description of Mary, Queen of Scots, written in 1955.

and differences. This is usually asked in the form of 'How far do Sources A and B agree about...' This requires you to analyse both sources and evaluate how far they agree or disagree in their presentation and interpretation of an issue. This kind of question is usually allocated six marks.

Answering cross-referencing of sources questions in practice

How far does the portrait (Source B) support the historian's description of Mary Stuart in Source A? Use the sources and your own knowledge to explain your answer. **[6 marks]**

SOURCE B

A portrait of Mary, Queen of Scots, painted in 1578. The original showed words in the top left corner that describe her as thirty-six years old, the Queen of Scotland, widow of the King of France, and a prisoner in England.

ACTIVITIES

1   To practise answering cross-referencing of sources questions, and in particular the question above, first copy and complete the table as a plan for your answer. Do this as a timed activity. Try spending 15 minutes answering the question to begin with. In this time, you should plan and write your answer. Then pass your answers to another student for them to grade according to the examiner's tips.

What do the sources show or infer about...?	Source A (give specific examples from the source)	Source B (give specific examples from the source)	Agree/disagree with each other
Beauty			
Intelligence			
Men's loyalty towards her			
A threat to Elizabeth I			
Reliability of the source taken from the attribution			

2   Now swap the sources for two more and identify your own issue to cross reference. By doing this activity, you will increase your speed at answering such questions, you will learn a routine and how to structure the questions, and you will also begin to think like an examiner and thus be better prepared for the exam.

GradeStudio

Examiner's tips

- Use the mark allocation as a guide to how many points you should make, how long you should take answering the question and roughly how long your answer should be.
- Read or study each source carefully, ensuring that you understand what you read, the **inferences** made and the imagery used.
- Read the question again to clarify the issue the examiner has identified as the focus of cross referencing. Do not simply write everything the sources agree on as it may be irrelevant.

- Point out general themes, attitudes and tones the sources may agree on.
- Support these with specific examples from the sources.
- The question asks you 'how far' the portrait supports the description. In other words you need to use your judgement to decide to what extent the portrait supports the description.
- Now conclude and give your judgement/opinion. If you can, explain why the sources differ by analysing the **attribution** of the source.
- Use the language of the question in your answer.

1.8 Did Elizabeth I show weaknesses and misjudgements in the way she dealt with Mary, Queen of Scots?

LEARNING OBJECTIVES

In this lesson you will:

- analyse whether Elizabeth I showed weaknesses and misjudgements in her dealings with Mary, Queen of Scots
- practise using source comprehension skills.

KEY WORDS

House arrest – *imprisoned but not in a prison. Putting Mary Stuart under house arrest meant that she could maintain full honour as a queen while being held captive.*

Mary the prisoner

As soon as Mary Stuart, Queen of Scots, rode into England in 1568, she was imprisoned. She was kept under **house arrest** at various houses and castles, mainly in Staffordshire, for the next 19 years. During this time, she and Elizabeth I, her cousin, never met.

Mary Stuart was seen by Catholics in England as the rightful ruler and became the focal point for plots and conspiracies:

- In 1569, the Northern Earls planned to seize Mary Stuart, march to London, place her on the throne of England and re-establish the Catholic religion.

- The Ridolfi Plot in 1571 planned the marriage of the Duke of Norfolk, a leading noble, to Mary Stuart and then planned to establish her as the queen with the promise of help from the King of Spain and the Pope.

- In 1583, in the Throckmorton Plot, English Catholics planned to rebel and place Mary Stuart on the throne with Spanish help.

The Babington Plot of 1586 left Elizabeth I little choice but to act against another queen. Babington and his men had planned to kill Elizabeth I and replace her with Mary Stuart. Unfortunately for Mary, her letter back to Babington approving the plot was intercepted by Elizabeth I's spies. It was clear evidence of her involvement in a plot to assassinate Elizabeth I. In October 1586, Mary was tried for 'imagining and encompassing Her Majesty's death'. Mary was executed on 8 February 1587 (see Source A).

Elizabeth I agreed to the execution eventually but only when she was able to shift the blame for it to parliament. She did her best to pacify James IV, after the execution of his mother, by completely disassociating herself from the final decision, which she left to the Privy Council. She insisted on a scapegoat and, as a result, William Davison, secretary to the Privy Council, who Elizabeth had entrusted the death warrant, was imprisoned. Throughout her reign, Elizabeth I had always claimed the sanctity of rulers against rebellion of their subjects. She was all too aware that such actions against another ruler could backfire and

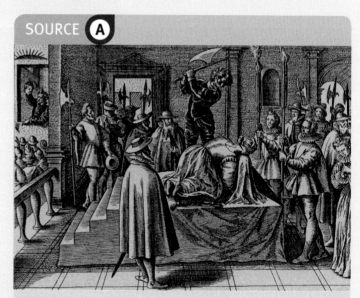

SOURCE A

The execution of Mary, Queen of Scots.

she could suffer the same fate. Fortunately, ballads were written and fires were lit in the streets to celebrate. Every Protestant in the country, including Elizabeth I, must have sighed with relief. The figurehead of years of plots and rebellions had now been removed.

SOURCE B

The Scottish Queen's life cannot stand with Her Majesty's safety and quiet estate of the realm, being as she is the only ground of all practices and attempts both at home and abroad. Mercy and Pity is nothing else but cruel kindness; but in the Scottish Queen experience teaches that the more favour she receives the more mischief she attempts. What dishonour were it, in sparing the life of so grievous an offender, to hazard the lives of so many thousands of true subjects, being left to so malicious a woman.

Sir Christopher Hatton, a Privy Councillor, 1586–87.

Did Elizabeth show weaknesses and misjudgements in the way she dealt with Mary, Queen of Scots?

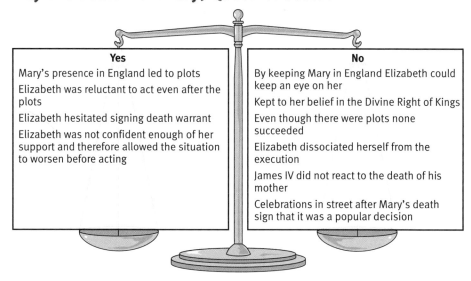

Yes
- Mary's presence in England led to plots
- Elizabeth was reluctant to act even after the plots
- Elizabeth hesitated signing death warrant
- Elizabeth was not confident enough of her support and therefore allowed the situation to worsen before acting

No
- By keeping Mary in England Elizabeth could keep an eye on her
- Kept to her belief in the Divine Right of Kings
- Even though there were plots none succeeded
- Elizabeth dissociated herself from the execution
- James IV did not react to the death of his mother
- Celebrations in street after Mary's death sign that it was a popular decision

SOURCE C

Mary Stuart was a free and absolute princess and had no superior but God alone… Elizabeth had kept her still in prison, and violated the sacred rights of hospitality; that she could not be other ways reputed than as a prisoner taken in war. She could not commit treason, because she was no subject, and Princes in equal degree have no power or sovereignty over one another. Moreover, that it was never heard of, that a Prince should be subjected to the stroke of an executioner.

William Camden, 1615.

SOURCE D

To endanger the completed alliance with Scotland or the goodwill of France, at a time when the great duel with Spain was looming over the horizon, was a heavy price to pay for ridding England of the enemy within the gate.

J.S. Black, *The Reign of Elizabeth I, 1558–1603*, 1936.

ACTIVITIES

1 Write a diary entry for Elizabeth I on the day of the execution of Mary, Queen of Scots. Remember, Elizabeth I was a great analytical thinker and so her thoughts on the matter would have been very serious and would have considered whether she thought her actions showed weaknesses or misjudgements.

   In order to help you do this, consider Sources B to D and the following:

   - How did Elizabeth I feel about the Divine Right of Kings? What risks was she running if she executed another queen? She was under considerable pressure to execute Mary Stuart from her Privy Council – did she show weakness, therefore, by giving into their pressure?

   - Elizabeth I's responsibility to the people of England – did she show misjudgement in keeping Mary Stuart alive so long? Did she show misjudgement in the people's loyalty towards her and in her legitimacy as queen?

   - What risks did Elizabeth I face with regard to the reaction of the Catholics at home and abroad if she executed a Catholic queen? Was it a misjudgement or a worthwhile risk?

2 Finish off Elizabeth I's diary entry by concluding whether you feel the execution exposed some weaknesses or misjudgements on your (Elizabeth I's) part.

1.9 Case study: Did Elizabeth I show weaknesses and misjudgements in the way she dealt with the Earl of Essex?

LEARNING OBJECTIVES

In this lesson you will:

- analyse Elizabeth I's dealings with the Earl of Essex for weaknesses and misjudgements.
- practise using source comprehension skills.

KEY WORDS

Favourites – *those Elizabeth gave special attention and rewards to.*

Monopoly – *total control, no competition on specified goods.*

Treason – *acting unlawfully against your country and your monarch.*

The Essex Rebellion

Elizabeth I relied on the patronage of her nobles and governing classes to keep order across the country. In return for profit and political advancement, she would receive loyalty and obedience. This led to intense competition among the Queen's **favourites**.

Robert Devereux, the Earl of Essex, was a firm favourite of Elizabeth in the later part of her reign. He was a charming and flamboyant character and it seems that Elizabeth I was flattered by his flirtatious behaviour. In 1598, there was a rebellion in Ireland led by Hugh O'Neill, the Earl of Tyrone. Elizabeth I chose the Earl of Essex to lead the campaign against this rebellion, making him Lord Lieutenant of Ireland and giving him the largest force ever sent to Ireland – 16,000 troops (see Source A).

The campaign was a disaster. Essex directly disobeyed orders to fight the Earl of Tyrone and, instead, agreed a treaty with him. Evidence would suggest that they each agreed to support the succession of James VI after Elizabeth I's death and then support each other claiming authority in their own country. Elizabeth was furious with her former favourite. Essex then made another mistake. He deserted his post in Ireland and came back to England to beg Elizabeth for her forgiveness. He was put under house arrest for over a year.

In 1600, Elizabeth I replaced Essex as Lord Lieutenant of Ireland with Lord Mountjoy, Charles Blount. With an army of 13,000, he defeated O'Neill. The defeat brought an end to Gaelic resistance to English rule in Ireland.

Essex's freedom was eventually given but the main source of his income, **monopoly** of the sale of sweet wine in England, originally granted by Elizabeth (see Source B) was removed. He was also banned from Court. He moved from 'sorrow and repentance to rage and rebellion'.

SOURCE A

The Earl of Essex. His interests lay largely in military expeditions. Although successful in Cadiz as a military commander, he failed to achieve anything in the expeditions he led against Spain in 1595 and 1597 and the campaign in Ireland was a disaster.

He conceived a wild and desperate plan to force an entry into the Privy Chamber, take control of Elizabeth and purge the Privy Council of the likes of Robert Cecil who he had fallen out with even though they both supported James VI as successor to Elizabeth (see Source C).

This initial plan was abandoned when it was learned that Elizabeth's guards had been doubled. Instead, on 7 February 1601, Essex arranged for a performance of Shakespeare's *Richard II* to be performed at the Globe Theatre, a play that revolved around Richard losing his throne after listening to ill-intentioned advisers. This was an obvious reference to Cecil and the next day four Privy Councillors were sent to Essex's house to summon him to court. The councillors were taken hostage and Essex, with 300 supporters and having tried but failed to gain the support of Lord Mountjoy in Ireland, set out into the city. The Earl of Nottingham was sent to arrest Essex and after a short skirmish was arrested.

The Earl of Essex was convicted of **treason** and sentenced to death on 25 February 1601. Elizabeth I was said to have cried for days after his death.

SOURCE C

Essex desperately turned his mind to a coup in the autumn of 1600. When Elizabeth refused to renew his patent of sweet wines in September, his credit structure collapsed. She had effectively condemned him to a life of poverty, nor would she answer his appeal for an audience... Creditors were pressing for payment and starting to arrest his servants who had stood surety for him. Yet Essex's motivation went beyond this. A faction leader who was denied access to the monarch was in an untenable position; the earl saw himself as compelled to act because his court opponents had exploited their 'corrupt' monopoly of power.

J. Guy, *Tudor England*, 1988.

SOURCE B

Viewed as a system of political patronage, Elizabethan government shows certain defects. It lacked adequate safeguards against a free for all scramble for spoils (rewards).... The nature of prizes (rewards) encouraged a reckless competition... They were... too small, and the incumbent (receiver) was driven to increase his income by any means open to him... The terms of appointment were in many cases ill defined... and this encouraged the office holder to exploit his opportunities... The private exploitation of political advantage created a vast 'black market' in which political influence and favour were increasingly bought and sold... The poverty of the crown drove it to make unwise concessions to suitors for favour or place. Grants of monopoly... were tempting to the crown because they offered an increase in income for no outlay.

W. MacCaffrey, in S.T. Bindoff, J. Hurstfield and C.H. Williams *Elizabethan Government and Society* 'Place and Patronage in Elizabethan Politics', 1961.

ACTIVITY

How well did Elizabeth deal with Essex?
The table outlines different points of view. Use your own knowledge and Sources B and C to explain the different points of view and whether they show Elizabeth dealt well with Essex or not.

Point of view	Explanation	Dealt well or not
Elizabeth could have supported Essex as a suitor and distant cousin but wanted to make an example of him to others		
The system of patronage in Elizabeth's Court was bound to create problems		
Elizabeth gave Essex no alternative but to act against her		
Essex out of the way allowed Robert Cecil to take full control of the Privy Council and led to James VI's succession two years later		
Seven of the Essex Rebellion plotters were convicted of the Gunpowder Plot in 1605		
Sending Lord Mountjoy to Ireland was successful		

1.10 How far had Elizabeth I achieved her aims by the end of her reign?

LEARNING OBJECTIVES

In this lesson you will:
- investigate how far Elizabeth I had achieved her aims by the end of her reign
- practise using source comprehension skills.

KEY WORDS

National identity – *a sense of what it is to belong to a country and be part of its characteristic features.*
Stability – *consistency, things remaining the same for some time giving the opportunity for them to settle.*

Gloriana

Edmund Spenser, the poet who wrote *The Faerie Queene*, was a Protestant and keen supporter of Elizabeth I. He wished to portray her in the best possible light, 'In that Faery Queen I mean glory in my general intention but in my particular I conceive the most excellent and glorious person of our sovereign…'. In Spenser's view the aims Elizabeth had at the start of her reign had been achieved. She had established herself as the rightful heir to the throne, she had become very popular amongst her people and she had ensured the safety and security of the kingdom. Her reign had also seen an increase in foreign trade and exploration and a flourishing of arts and culture.

However her entitlement to this high praise has been hotly debated by historians ever since. What is without doubt is that after the short reigns of her brother and sister, her 45 years on the throne provided valuable **stability** for the kingdom and helped forge a sense of **national identity**.

SOURCE A

Elizabeth died unloved and almost unlamented, and it was partly her own fault. She had aimed for popularity and political security by projecting herself as the ever young and ever beautiful virgin mother of her people, bringing them peace and prosperity; she ended her days as an irascible old woman, presiding over war and failure abroad and poverty and factionalism at home… The world in which Elizabeth had painstakingly built her model of female monarchy changed – but Elizabeth lived up to her motto, semper eadem, always the same. She was a ruler overtaken by events.

Modern historian, C. Haigh, in *Elizabeth I*, published in 1998, who famously reconsidered the successes of Elizabeth I and has influenced some other historians' views.

SOURCE B

Elizabeth I, c.1600, unknown artist.

SOURCE C

To be a king and wear a crown is a thing more glorious to them that see it, than it is pleasant to them that bear it. For myself, I was never so much enticed with the glorious name of a king or royal authority of a queen, as delighted that God hath made me His instrument to maintain His truth and glory, and to defend this Kingdom from peril, dishonour, tyranny and oppression. There will never a queen sit in my seat with more zeal to my country, care to my subjects, and that will sooner with willingness venture her life for your good and safety, than myself.

Elizabeth I's speech to Parliament, 1601, summarising the achievements of her reign as her popularity was beginning to wane.

SOURCE D

She tried hard to heal the wounds and divisions of the England she inherited, and she met with a large measure of success... In her public tasks she succeeded admirably during the first thirty years of her reign in healing the wounds and binding the nation to her own purposes; but she failed significantly during the last fifteen. Delay, ambiguity, the elevation of the monarchy to raise the aims and unify the purpose of the Elizabethan people were no longer enough. In one sense her reign was both too long and too short. If she had lived ten years less she might have gone down in history as the most successful monarch to sit on the English throne.

J. Hurstfield, *The Elizabethan Nation*, 1964.

SOURCE E

That line of statesmen-monarchs than whom, indeed, no wiser or mightier ever adorned the English throne, and of whom she herself... was in the fullness of her genius the superb and matchless flower.

S.T. Bindoff, *Tudor England*, written in 1950 in a post-Second World War period of revival in Britain similar to that of the Elizabethan era.

ACTIVITIES

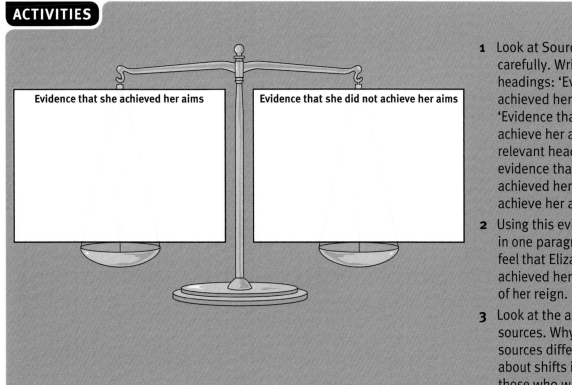

Evidence that she achieved her aims

Evidence that she did not achieve her aims

1 Look at Sources A to E carefully. Write down the headings: 'Evidence that she achieved her aims' and 'Evidence that she did not achieve her aims'. Under the relevant headings provide evidence that Elizabeth I achieved her aims/did not achieve her aims.

2 Using this evidence, conclude in one paragraph how far you feel that Elizabeth I had achieved her aims by the end of her reign.

3 Look at the attribution of the sources. Why do you think the sources differ so much? Think about shifts in emphasis of those who wrote the sources.

You have now completed this unit which has focused on the success of Elizabeth I's reign. You have also had practice answering questions that will help you prepare for your examination. Below is a typical examination question on evaluating the success of Elizabeth I throughout her reign.

Source A

Oh Lord God, most merciful Father, who as upon this day, placing thy servant our sovereign and gracious queen Elizabeth in the kingdom, didst deliver thy people of England from the danger of war and oppression, both of bodies by tyranny and of conscience by superstition, restoring peace and true religion, with liberty both of bodies and minds, and hast continued the same thy blessings, without all desert on our part, now by the space of these eighteen years...

A Protestant prayer from 1576.

Study Source A. Are you surprised at the attitude towards the successes of Elizabeth I shown in the source? Use the source and your own knowledge to explain your answer. **[6 marks]**

Fact file

In your GCSE examination, you may be asked to make comments on an attitude on the period you are studying. This could be from the past or a modern interpretation. This kind of question is asking you to combine your source comprehension skills with your empathy skills. It is demanding that you separate modern viewpoints from those of the past. You must be able to set viewpoints of the past into their historical context. This sort of question is usually worth 6 marks.

Examiner's tips

- Use the mark allocation as a guide to how many points you should make, how long you should take answering the question and roughly how long your answer should be.
- Firstly, take time to understand the viewpoint being expressed and make a judgement on whether you are surprised or not.
- Explain the context of this sort of attitude – if it is modern, then think about sources of evidence that may have come to light, censorships that may have been removed, patterns that can now be identified through time, and of course the gift of hindsight.
- Then explain the context of this attitude specifically.

Before you have a go at a question like this, first read this simplified examiner mark scheme.

Simplified mark scheme

Level	Description of answer	Mark
Level 0	No evidence submitted or does not address the question	0
Level 1	Unsupported assertions/answers that fail to address the sources or answers based on everyday empathy	1
Level 2	Valid assertions about not being surprised/surprised or a statement of knowledge that would suggest they were not surprised/surprised	2
Level 3	Uses knowledge of the period to explain one contextual reason why they are not surprised/surprised but does not include attitudes	3
Level 4	Uses knowledge of the period to explain one contextual reason why they are not surprised/surprised (must include attitudes)	4–5
Level 5	Uses knowledge of the period to explain two contextual reasons why they are not surprised/surprised – at least one reason must be an attitude	6

Secondly, look at the sample student answer below – noting the examiner's comment.

Candidate's answer

I am not surprised by the attitude towards the successes of Elizabeth I shown in Source A. It is a Protestant prayer and Elizabeth I was a supporter of the Protestant religion, so allowing Protestants to practise their religion without fear of intimidation. This had not been the case during the rule of Elizabeth's half-sister, Mary, who had been a Catholic and had persecuted Protestants.

Examiner's comment

This candidate has reached a Level 3 answer. They use their contextual historical knowledge to explain one reason why they are not surprised by the contents of the prayer.

You can see from the mark scheme that in order to secure a Level 4 mark the answer needs to be specific about the attitudes shown. It would have to explain how people believed loyalty to the Queen was bound to loyalty to God. The source is written by someone who believes Protestantism is the true religion and that the Queen is a blessing from God. A Level 5 answer would explain two contextual reasons, one being an attitude.

Source B

This very woman, having seized on the kingdom and monstrously usurped the place of supreme head of the church in all England, and the chief authority and juriduction thereof, hath again reduced the said Kingdom into a miserable and ruinous condition, which was so lately reclaimed to the Catholic faith and a thriving condition. We seeing that wicked actions are multiplied one upon the other, as also the persecution of the faithful growth every day heavier by the means of Elizabeth.

Papal Bull of Excommunication, 1570.

Study Source B. Are you surprised at the attitude towards the legitimacy and successes of Elizabeth I? Use the source and your own knowledge to explain your answer. **[6 marks]**

Chapter 2

What was the importance of religion in Elizabethan England?

Before 1558

By the Act of Supremacy in 1534, Henry VIII became the recognised Supreme Head of the Church in England rather than the Pope. This gave him power to 'visit, repress, redress, reform, order, correct, restrain and amend all such errors, heresies, abuses, offences, contempts, and enormities, whatsoever they be'. Although he exploited the finances of the Church, his actual religious reforms were moderate and Catholic practices remained largely intact.

During Edward VI's very short reign, under the leadership of his regents, he undertook a Protestant Reformation. However, the evidence suggests that many people remained Catholic.

As a result, his successor Mary I had little difficulty reinstating Catholic practices. Her persecution of Protestants created martyrs and forced many into exile where they came into contact with advanced Protestant ideas. When Elizabeth I came to the throne in 1558, the religious situation was very complicated and her decisions would prove to be key to the peace in England and abroad.

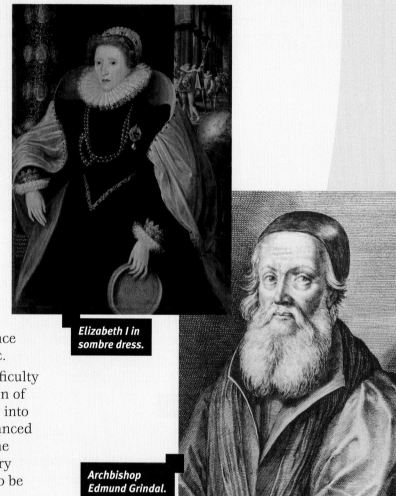

Elizabeth I in sombre dress.

Archbishop Edmund Grindal.

TIMELINE

Elizabeth I ascended the throne of England

Mary Stuart, Queen of Scots, a Catholic, escaped Scotland to England and was placed under house arrest

1555 — 1560 — 1565 — 1570

Act of Supremecy, Act of Uniformity and Royal Injunctions set out how the Church would be organised

Advertisements published laying down rules for clerical dress to settle vestments controversy. William Fulke expelled from St John's College, Cambridge for persuading college to discard the surplice

Defeat of the Rebellion of the Northern Earls to depose Elizabeth I and replace her with Mary, Queen of Scots

See heere the fface of Romes renowned ffoe,
Graue, larned, Fulk, whose worth his works, best shou...

**William Fulke,
prominent Puritan.**

After 1603

Even at the end of Elizabeth I's reign, many ordinary men and women, although converted to the Elizabethan national Church, understood very little of its religious teaching. As Elizabeth I's religious changes were compromises, they embraced some elements of Catholic and Protestant teachings and so left some subjects confused. Religious compromise also meant that there was little opportunity for radical change and so some, particularly Puritans, were disappointed by missed opportunities to rid the country of Catholics altogether.

As a result, disagreements between Puritan and Protestant ministers continued into the reigns of James I and Charles I. The religious reforms they introduced contributed to the causes of the civil war.

PIVS IV. Ioannes Angelus Mediceus, Mediolanen. creatus die 26. Decembr. an. 1559. Sed. an. 5. men. ii. dies 15. Obijt die 9. Decemb. an. 1565. Vac. Sed. dies 29.

Pope Pius IV.

**Mary Stuart,
Queen of Scotland.**

ACTIVITY

It is 1558 and you are about to leave school. You are considering going into the Church as your profession. This the same year that Elizabeth I comes to the throne – so will you choose the Catholic or Protestant Church?

Consider the following questions:

- What religion will the Church be under Elizabeth I?
- How will this religion have been chosen?
- What if you do not want to be part of this religion? Is there room for your own religious beliefs?
- What will be the consequences of the religious decisions made by the new queen?

Defeat of the Ridolfi Plot to depose Elizabeth I with an invasion from the Spanish Netherlands

Archbishop Grindal refused to obey royal orders to suppress prophesying

Jesuit priests arrived in England

1570 — 1575 — 1580 — 1585

Elizabeth I was excommunicated by Pope Pius IV

Arrival of the Douai priests

Defeat of the Throckmorton Plot to overthrow Elizabeth I with a combined force of English and French Catholics

2.1 Why did Elizabethans regard religion as important?

In this lesson you will:

- understand the role of the Church in Elizabethan society
- develop source comprehension skills.

Religion played an enormous role in the lives of Elizabethan men, women and children. Almost everyone believed in God, went to church on Sunday and took Communion at least once a year. They also expected to go to either Heaven or Hell. The Church provided order and gave guidance on everyday living outlining clear boundaries they should live and work within. It gave structure to parents on how they should bring up their children. During the Elizabethan era it gave out charity, called alms, to the poor. The Church was the main source of schooling. Hardly anyone apart from the clergy could read or write. The universities with their libraries were part of the Church. It was the centre of a village or town's community providing opportunities for feasts and holidays when saint's days or other religious events were celebrated. More importantly, in a time when doctors were expensive and their medical knowledge very limited, people turned to religion to seek cures for diseases like smallpox and dysentery.

Impact of the Renaissance

The Italian Renaissance or 'rebirth' spread to England during the Elizabethan era. It was a period of new ideas and new thinking across Europe. It saw the introduction of the printing press which helped bring about a renewed interest in all matters of religion including the supernatural. The renewed interest in the supernatural and witchcraft resulted in the Catholic Church expanding their definition of what constituted witchcraft and even those who innocently used herbal remedies became labelled witches. In 1562, Queen Elizabeth passed new harsher witchcraft laws 'Against Conjuracions Inchauntmentes and Witchecraftes'. During Elizabeth's reign there were 247 witchcraft trials.

SOURCE A

Drawing made in 1579. God is at the top, surrounded by angels. At the bottom, in hell, are the Devil and his demons, busy tormenting people. The saints are above the clouds. Below them are human beings – Europeans on the right and other people on the left. Then come birds, fish, animals and plants in order.

An old cheese all mouldy, mixed with water from an oiled salt gammon of bacon and applied as a poultice, doth soften all the hard swelling of the knees.

Elizabethan recipe for rheumatism.

SOURCE C

The number of witches and sorcerers has become enormous.

Comment by an English bishop in 1559.

Mixing patriotic and religious sentiments

As a result of the intense work done to promote Queen Elizabeth as the saviour of Protestantism, people's feelings of loyalty to the Queen were wrapped up with their worship of God. The Church promoted this idea, not only to ensure obedience and loyalty but it made it impossible for those who went against Elizabeth to portray themselves as religious martyrs. It also gave Elizabeth a degree of control over the minds of people.

What were Elizabeth's religious views?

Historians have debated what religious beliefs Elizabeth I really held. There is significant evidence at the beginning of her reign to suggest that she was Protestant. Elizabeth I had been educated by William Grindal, Roger Ascham, Sir Anthony Denny and Catherine Parr, all Protestants. She was therefore heavily influenced by the Protestant religion. Throughout the reign of her Catholic sister, Mary I, she had dressed in simple Protestant-style robes. She had also translated some important Protestant teachings and had continually used the English Bible in preference to the Latin version favoured by Catholics.

SOURCE D

I heartily pray the Almighty God to send a long, prosperous and happy life and reign to our good Queen Elizabeth and send us all grace that we may all live in his fear as good and dutiful subjects to our said gracious sovereign lady and queen, and all die before the sorrowful days of England shall come if God take her from us before the end of the world. And for that if for our sins he shorten her days, as he did the days of good King Edward, and yet he will grant me the grace to die at her feet before her, and that at the end of all things which is at hand we may joyfully rise again to life everlasting with perpetual joy and felicity.

Amen! Amen!

A prayer in the front page of the family Bible of a Sussex lawyer, 1585.

SOURCE E

When I first took the sceptre, my title made me not forget the giver, and therefore (I) began, as became me, with such religion as both I was born in, bred in, and, I trust, shall die in.

Elizabeth I, 1586.

ACTIVITIES

1 Copy and complete the speech bubbles describing five ways in which the Church was so important to ordinary people's lives. Use the text and the sources to help you.

2 Using your answer to question 1, explain why the Elizabethan authorities were so keen to quell any instances of witchcraft.

2.2 What was Elizabeth I trying to achieve through her religious settlement?

LEARNING OBJECTIVES

In this lesson you will:

- study the religious changes that Elizabeth I made on her accession to the throne of England and why she made them
- develop an understanding of the past through analysis of continuity and change and its significance within its historical context.

KEY WORDS

Compromise – *a settlement of a dispute in which two or more sides agree to accept less than they originally wanted.*
Erastian – *somebody who believes that the state has authority over the Church in ecclesiastical matters.*
JP – *Justice of Peace.*
Puritans – *Protestants who placed emphasis on preaching and wanted plain churches and no ceremonies.*
Surplice – *the white tunic usually worn by Catholic clergy.*

The religious settlement of 1559

Elizabeth I acted on matters of religion almost immediately because she understood the issues that could arise if she did not act quickly enough. One potential danger was that Catholics did not accept her as the rightful queen. Another was that Protestants might rebel over their treatment during the Catholic reign of her half-sister, Mary I. Elizabeth passed the Religious Settlement in 1559. This settlement was made up of the Act of Supremacy, the Act of Uniformity and the Royal Injunctions (see below). This Elizabethan church settlement is the basis of the Church of England that exists today.

The Religious Settlement was a careful **compromise** that reflected the personal religious

GETTING STARTED

Have you ever heard of the saying 'you can't please all of the people all of the time'? Sometimes changes can be seen as good and bad depending on who you are and what your situation and beliefs are. Discuss this with a partner and list a few examples of changes, consequences and who the changes affected in a good way and in a bad way. Can you think of a change that has happened that has pleased everyone involved?

beliefs of the Queen, but also showed her political awareness at home and abroad, and her ability to win the loyalty of her subjects.

The Act of Supremacy

Elizabeth I made herself Supreme Governor of the Church of England, rather than Supreme Head of the Church of England

All priests and lay people had to swear an oath of loyalty to Elizabeth I as Governor of the Church of England

Repealed the heresy laws

Guaranteed freedom of worship for Protestants

At Communion the worshippers would receive both the wine and the bread

The Act of Uniformity

New book of Common Prayer to be used in all churches and penalties for those refusing to use it

Everyone was to attend church on Sundays and holy days, if they didn't they were fined

Church ornaments and dress to be the same as in the early reign of Edward VI, in other words, plain

The Royal Injunctions

Every Church had to have a Bible written in English

All preachers had to have a licence and had to preach at least once a month

Pilgrimages were banned

At communion, kneeling was no longer forbidden and wafers could be used

There should be a pulpit and alms chest in every church

Clergy might marry with consent of bishop and two JPs

Clergy to wear the **surplice**

Record of births, marriages and deaths to be kept

The Settlement was designed to appease both Catholics and Protestants and create a church that appealed to the majority. Elizabeth had seen the religious unrest in France and the Netherlands and wanted to avoid this happening in England. It was a very clever piece of diplomacy but continued to be challenged by Catholics and **Puritans** who wished to modify or overthrow the Settlement. The Settlement reflected Elizabeth I's beliefs about monarchy and the roles and responsibilities of the ruler. As her father had done before her, Elizabeth I ensured that not only did she hold political power but she held full religious power too – **Erastian** power.

Fact file

Puritans believed that churches and indeed the priests should be decorated as simply as possible so that nothing distracted those praying to God. They wanted services, the prayer book and the Bible to be accessible to the general laity (ordinary people) so people could think and question for themselves. There were some radical preachers who spread some radical ideas among the people. For example, they wanted to see every congregation running its own church with a group of elders. They believed that at communion, the offerings represented Christ, while Catholics believed that the wine and bread were *actually* the blood and body of Christ.

Catholics believed in pilgrimages and that churches and priests should be decorated as finely as possible to display their commitment to God. They also felt that the prayer book and the Bible should be in Latin and that the laity should not question religious teachings. They firmly believed in the authority of bishops and archbishops and ultimately the Pope. They did not accept Elizabeth I as the Supreme Governor of the Church in England.

  GradeStudio

Explanation and analysis

How far did the Religious Settlement of 1559 satisfy both the Puritans and the Catholics?

In order to tackle this question, copy and complete the table below.

1 Complete columns 2 and 3 – how did the Catholics and Puritans feel about the major religious issues that needed to be settled?
2 Complete column 4 – how did Elizabeth I act upon each issue through passing the Religious Settlement?
3 Complete column 5 – finally, evaluate how both the Puritans and the Catholics would have reacted to each royal instruction.

Area of concern	What did the Catholics believe should happen?	What did the Puritans believe should happen?	What did Elizabeth I instruct on this matter in the Religious Settlement of 1559?	How would Catholics and Puritans have reacted to this?
The Head of the Church in England				
Structure of the management of the Church				
Decoration of churches and priests				
Access to prayer books and the Bible				
Communion and preaching				

2.3 How great a threat were the Catholics from abroad?

LEARNING OBJECTIVES

In this lesson you will:

- learn about the threat posed to Elizabeth I by Catholics from abroad
- practise using source comprehension skills.

KEY WORDS

Spanish Armada – *the Spanish fleet of ships sent to overthrow Protestant rule in England.*

England and Europe

The issue of religion was linked closely to foreign affairs:

- In the eyes of Catholic Europe, Elizabeth I was the illegitimate child of Henry VIII. To turn England into a Catholic country would be for Elizabeth to agree with Catholic Europe that she was not the rightful heir to the throne.
- On the other hand, England as a Protestant country could lead to disastrous relations with powerful Catholic nations in Europe and ultimately to war.
- England was an ally of Catholic Spain in the war against France. The war ended in 1559. England could not afford to fight the war alone.
- King Philip II of Spain persuaded the Pope that England could be won back to Catholicism by peaceful means.
- Spain was involved in the Dutch Rebellion 1566–1609 in the Spanish Netherlands. This cost money, soldiers and time. Philip II was worried that if Elizabeth I was taken from the throne, she would be replaced by her Catholic cousin, who had been Queen of France, an enemy of Spain.
- In Italy, the leadership of the Pope was weak until around 1570. Until this time the Catholic threat from overseas appeared to be minimal.

A change in circumstances

Throughout her reign Elizabeth was acutely aware that Catholics abroad were a significant threat. Her greatest fear was that the largest and most powerful Catholic nations (France and Spain) would join together in a 'Catholic Alliance' to launch an attack on Protestant England.

France was involved in religious civil wars from 1562 to 1598 which acted as a distraction from involvement in foreign affairs. With the disturbances in the Netherlands and a worsening of relations with Spain, Elizabeth saw an opportunity to improve relations with France and the Treaty of Blois was signed by France and England in 1572 which stated that the two countries would promise to help each other if Spain attacked either of them. However, in 1584, the French Catholic League and Spain signed the Treaty of Joinville in which Philip II of Spain promised to help disinherit the Protestant Henry of Navarre (the future Henry IV) in favour of the Catholic Henry of Guise. Learning of this treaty, Elizabeth again feared a 'Catholic Alliance' and sent help to Henry of Navarre to secure the throne in France.

Elizabeth also began to help the Dutch rebels against Philip II of Spain which in turn gave Spain a reason to help English Catholics remove Elizabeth from the throne, a policy known throughout Catholic Europe as Empresa de Inglaterra (the Enterprise of England) and in 1588, the **Spanish Armada** planned an invasion of England from the Netherlands.

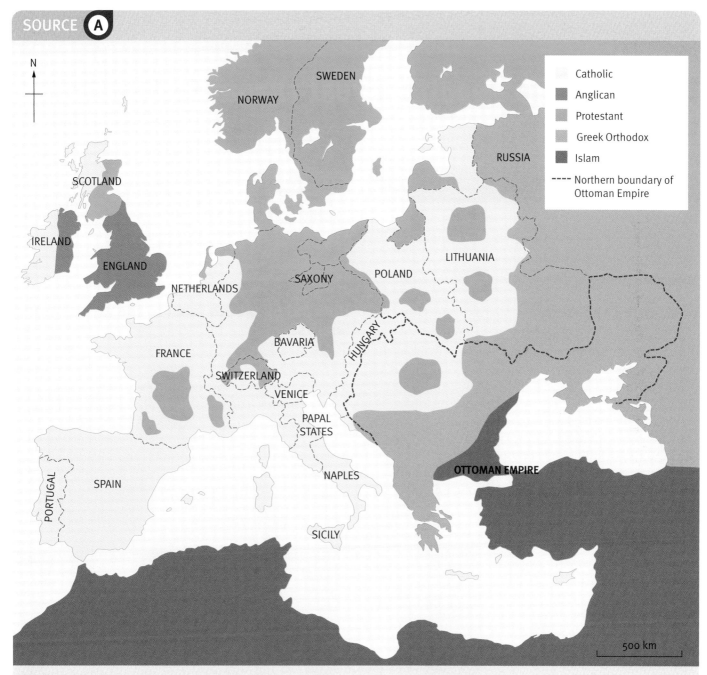

N

Religious and political divisions in Europe, 1559.

ACTIVITIES

1 How real a threat was the 'Catholic Alliance' that Elizabeth feared so much? Use the information and Source A.

2 How far would you agree that Elizabethan foreign policy was Elizabethan religious policy? Explain your answer.

2.4 Were the Jesuits a real threat to Elizabeth I?

LEARNING OBJECTIVES

In this lesson you will:

- learn about the threat posed by the Jesuits
- practise giving full explanations.

KEY WORDS

Jesuits – *members of the 'Society of Jesus' founded by Ignatius Loyola in 1534. They were similar to monks but were able to travel to promote Catholicism.*

Who were the Jesuits?

The **Jesuits** were a Catholic order of priests founded by St Ignatius Loyola in 1534 to help in the fight against the Reformation begun by Elizabeth's father, Henry VIII. In 1540 they came under the direction of the Pope. From 1580 they began to arrive in England. Their aim was to not only keep the Catholic faith alive, but to convert the whole of England to Catholicism. They rejected any compromise whatsoever of the Catholic faith and were the arch enemies of anti-Catholic beliefs.

How did Elizabeth react to the arrival of the Jesuits?

Elizabeth had been determined not to offend Catholics too severely with her conservative religious changes. The compromises she introduced were to ensure the Catholic traditional sections of her people did not become alienated and rebel. However, the arrival of the Jesuits and the seminary priests from Douai (see page 40) in the Netherlands changed all this. In 1581 Elizabeth passed the 'Act to Retain the Queen's Majesty's Subjects in their

SOURCE

Jesuits were tortured until they surrendered and said they had been involved in plots to overthrow the Queen. In this way Elizabeth could execute them for treason rather than heresy which would have made them martyrs.

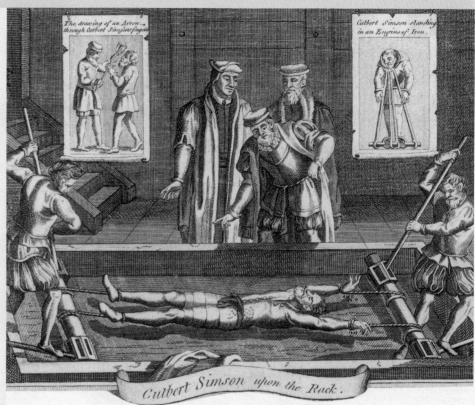

True Obedience' and the 'Act Against Seditious Words and Rumours' aimed specifically at the arrival of the priests. The response from the Pope was to send even more Jesuit priests and so in 1585 Elizabeth passed the 'Act Against Jesuits, Seminary Priests and such other Disobedient Persons'. This meant Catholic priests ordained since 1585 were given 40 days to leave the country. If they stayed they were sentenced to death for high treason. During this period 146 Catholic priests were executed and 10 Jesuit priests, mostly under this Act. In 1592 and 1602 Royal Proclamations established Commissioners to search out and find Catholic priests, in particular Jesuits.

Who was Edmund Campion?

Edmund Campion (see Source B) and Robert Parsons were the first Jesuit priests to arrive in England. Campion became a Jesuit in 1573 and after a time in Prague entered London in 1580 disguised as a jewel merchant. As soon as he began to preach the authorities started to search him out. He concentrated his ministering work in Lancashire, Oxfordshire, Northamptonshire and Berkshire. He wrote a book called 'Ten Reasons' against the Anglican Church and secretly gave out free copies. The book created a great deal of interest making it increasingly important for the authorities to hunt Campion down. He was eventually captured and presented before Elizabeth who offered him the opportunity to renounce his faith but he refused. He was hung, drawn and quartered on 1 December 1581. He was eventually made a saint.

Why was Elizabeth so worried by the Jesuits?

During the first 15 years of Elizabeth's reign the Catholics were leaderless. This allowed Elizabeth to make changes with little opposition. When the Jesuits landed in England the situation changed. The Jesuits were intelligent, well educated and highly motivated and would not err from their aim.

They deliberately courted the English gentry who had Catholic leanings. With their big houses the gentry were able to provide safe havens for the priests in secret rooms called priest holes. The Jesuit presence in England forced Elizabeth to take a harder approach to Catholics than she would have liked and in spite of the many deaths the Catholic faith survived. The dedication and commitment of the Jesuits had revived Catholic resistance against the religious reforms of Elizabeth.

SOURCE **B**

Portrait of Edmund Campion and in the background showing him being drawn and quartered.

GradeStudio

Recall and select knowledge

Why did Elizabeth's government fear the Jesuits so much? Explain your answer. **(7 marks)**

Examiner's tip

In order to produce a good answer you must use specific historical knowledge of the period and give explanations of at least two reasons.

2.5 The threat from the Catholics at home

LEARNING OBJECTIVES

In this lesson you will:
- learn about the threat of the Catholics at home
- practise using source comprehension skills.

The Pope and Catholics in England

The Pope was slow to give guidance to Catholics in England about how they should act towards their new queen and her religious changes. However, in the Council of Trent in 1562, it did say that Catholics should not attend Protestant services and in 1566 Pope Pius V forbade church attendance. Elizabeth was worried that a separated Catholic Church was being encouraged with allegiance only to Rome. Even those Catholic priests who claimed to conform to Elizabeth's new Church of England kept Catholic rituals and practices alive much to her annoyance. Elizabeth hoped the Catholic Church in England would gradually disappear and chose not to persecute the Catholics but to encourage conformity instead. Penalties were lenient, and she refused to make martyrs of Catholics and preferred to imprison them instead. Nonetheless, despite her calm exterior Elizabeth considered the Catholics in England to be a severe threat to national security.

Conspiracies, plots and rebellions

In 1568 Mary Stuart fled to England. Many Catholics saw her as the rightful ruler of England and so she became the focus of many conspiracies.

The Northern Rebellion, 1569

In 1562 French Catholics took control of Paris and murdered French Protestants. This made Elizabeth increasingly worried about her lack of control of the northern parts of England, near to Catholic Scotland. She therefore replaced the authority of the northern nobles with that of handpicked southern nobles who she felt she could trust. Nobles such as the Earl of Northumberland who lost their family lands in this way, now had no reason to remain loyal to Elizabeth. The Earls of Northumberland and Westmorland and Lord Leonard Dacre, planned first

to free Mary, Queen of Scots from her house arrest in England. Once this was done they had two options: they could use Mary to force Elizabeth I to make concessions on religion and name her as successor; or they could depose Elizabeth I and replace her with Mary immediately.

To help the rebellion the Pope was asked to issue a decree (Papal Bull) to excommunicate Elizabeth from the Catholic Church. It was hoped this would encourage Catholics to join the rebels (see Source A).

At the same time there was an interconnected plot in Elizabeth's court in London to allow the Duke of Norfolk (who had Catholic sympathies) to marry Mary, Queen of Scots. The plan was suggested by the Earl of Leicester (Robert Dudley), one of Elizabeth's court favourites, and had Catholic support from the Earl of Westmorland, who was the Duke of Norfolk's brother-in-law, and the Earl of Northumberland. The marriage, they hoped would allow Mary to gain popularity at court.

SOURCE A

The Pope excommunicating the Queen, talking to the Northern Earls.

Failure of the plan

- The Earl of Leicester confessed to the plots.
- Elizabeth I moved Mary, Queen of Scots from London so that she could not be the figurehead of the rebellion.
- The Papal Bull did not arrive until after the rebellion had collapsed.
- The rebels were pushed northwards by the Earl of Sussex and his troops of the Council of the North with little resistance.

With the collapse of the rebellion, Elizabeth I ordered the deaths of 700 rebels including the Earl of Northumberland. The Duke of Norfolk was imprisoned in the tower awaiting his fate.

The Rudolfi Plot, 1571

Roberto Ridolfi had been involved in the plot of the Rebellion of the Northern Earls. He had learned from the mistakes of that plot that foreign help was needed to depose Elizabeth. Through his connections as a Florentine banker, he secured the help of the Spanish Duke of Alba and 10,000 soldiers who were stationed in the Netherlands. Ridolfi overestimated the English support he would receive. Unfortunately, part of his plan was to replace Elizabeth with Mary Stuart and for Mary to marry the Duke of Norfolk. Mary, being a former Queen of France, made it impossible for the Duke of Alba to support this part of the plan as he feared it would lead to a powerful union of France and England, so backed off. Word of the plot reached Elizabeth. Although there was evidence to connect Mary Stuart to the plot Elizabeth did not have her executed. Ridolfi was never captured as he remained abroad for the rest of his life but the Duke of Norfolk was executed.

The Throckmorton Plot, 1583

Sir Francis Throckmorton acted as an intermediary between the imprisoned Mary Stuart, the Spanish Ambassador and Catholic supporters. Elizabeth's spies arrested and tortured him and he admitted to being involved in planning a Catholic uprising to depose Elizabeth. Although he retracted his statement later he was accused of high treason and executed.

The Babington Plot, 1586

A Catholic, Gilbert Gifford, had been captured and when tortured by Elizabeth's spies confessed to a planned plot to kill the Queen and replace her with Mary. Walsingham, Elizabeth's chief spy agreed to free the man if he acted as a double agent. He duly began passing letters between the other conspirators including Mary Stuart and Anthony Babington, a Catholic with connections at the French embassy, outlining the plot. However, every letter that passed through his hands he shared with Walsingham. As a result all details of the planned assassination were revealed. Babington was hung drawn and quartered (see Source B) and there was at last solid evidence to bring Mary Stuart to trial and she was sentenced to death for treason.

SOURCE B

Hanging of the conspirators in the Babington Plot.

ACTIVITY

You are responsible for Queen Elizabeth's publicity. There has been much talk about the recent plots and rebellions and it is your job to make sure the right message gets out to the people of England. That message is that the Queen will not tolerate rebellion; she is a loving Queen but will deal with those that rebel firmly; Catholics need to conform. Write a four minute discussion of the information that supports this statement. Consider the following:

- What are the common themes of the plots?
- How big a threat were the plots?
- Did the punishments fit the crimes?
- What impact did the plots and their outcomes have on the people of England and their religious choices?

2.6 How successful was Elizabeth I in combating Catholicism?

LEARNING OBJECTIVES

In this lesson you will:
- understand how successful Elizabeth was in dealing with the Catholics
- practise evaluating a historical source.

Catholicism in England

Following the Catholic reign of her sister, Mary I, much of England was Catholic. However, by the end of Elizabeth I's reign the number of Catholics had declined significantly, accounting for 1 or 2 per cent of the population. How far was this due to the actions of Elizabeth? How far was it due to the inactions of the Pope? How far was it due to the natural decrease in the number of Catholic priests and to internal factions within the Catholic faith? Read the sources below and decide for yourself.

SOURCE B

While in the short term the government's avoidance of confrontation with the Catholics allowed Catholicism to survive throughout the country during the 1560s, in the longer term it helped to ensure its eventual failure, as few felt pressured into resistance or rebellion before 1569. As a result the Elizabethan regime had time to establish itself, accustom many men and women to the new church and win over the Conservative landowners... As a consequence, few Catholics felt the need to separate from the established church in the 1560s, and many slipped into conformity or conversion... In reality the danger from English Catholics was exaggerated. The vast majority of them were loyal to their Queen and country and simply hoped for better times when the Catholic Mary Stuart would succeed to the throne. The Northern Rebellion was largely contained within the northern counties... And there was no sign of Catholic revolt in counties like Hampshire where Catholicism was strong during these troubled years.

S. Doran, *Elizabeth I and Religion*, 1994.

KEY WORDS

Douai missionaries – *Jesuit priests. The University of Douai was founded by Philip II of Spain in 1426. Douai is in present-day France but it was once part of the Spanish Netherlands. It was where Jesuit priests trained.*

SOURCE A

When the parish priest was ready to use the Book of Common Prayer and the Squire publicly appeared at the new services, it was hardly surprising that the ordinary people followed the examples of their social superiors.

P. McGrath, *Papists and Puritans under Elizabeth I*, 1967.

VOICE YOUR OPINION!

Discuss how it must have felt to be a Catholic at this time in England.

Would you have been prepared to give up your faith to save you and your family from possible death?

Discuss how the Catholic/Protestant situation in Elizabethan England is similar/different to modern day conflicts between different religions.

The Book of Common Prayer *published in 1552.*

*The effect of the **Douai missionaries** was paradoxical. The mission redefined the distinctive features of Catholicism which, after the initial resistance to the settlement, had been in danger of becoming blurred. Catholicism therefore retained a separate identity and did not simply disappear into the Church of England. But the process, because it was politicised, alienated almost all those who had once been Catholic. The more blurred the identity of the Catholic Church had been, the more adherents it had retained. The sharper the focus became, the more adherents the Catholic Church lost.*

S. Lee, *The Reign of Elizabeth I, 1558–1603*, 2007.

The situation for Catholics was not helped by the Papal Bull of 1570. By forbidding Catholics to attend English church services, the Pope made them face fines, which many could not afford to pay. They also felt forced into a choice between loyalty to their friends, neighbours and the state or to their Church; few were prepared to put the latter first.

N. Fellowes, *Elizabeth I*, 2004.

ACTIVITIES

1 Look at all the sources carefully. Copy and complete the table below. For each source look at what contribution Elizabeth made to the decline of Catholicism in England and the contribution made by other factors such as lack of leadership from the Pope in Source A.

Source	Explain how Elizabeth's action caused the decline of the Catholic Church	Explain how other factors caused the decline of the Catholic Church
A		
B		
C		
D		

2 In your opinion how effective was Elizabeth at forcing the decline of the Catholic Church in England? Explain your answer using the completed table.

What was the importance of religion in Elizabethan England? 41

2.7 What threat to Elizabeth I did the Puritans pose?

LEARNING OBJECTIVES

In this lesson you will:
- learn about the threat posed by the Puritans
- practise using source comprehension skills.

KEY WORDS

Admonitions – *mild but earnest criticisms.*

Marian exiles – *Protestant priests who had been exiled during the Catholic reign of Queen Mary I.*

SOURCE A

The Queen complained of '... diversity, variety, contention and vain love of singularity in her church' and urged Parker and the Bishops to take instant action 'so as uniformity of order may be kept in every church'. Parker was told to ensure that ecclesiastical livings were only served by men who promised 'to observe, keep and maintain... order and uniformity in all the external rites and ceremonies'

Letter of complaint from Elizabeth I to the Archbishop of Canterbury, 25 January 1565 (adapted).

Who were the Puritans?

Generally the Puritans were from the more educated sections of society, such as lawyers and skilled workers. They were extreme Protestants who wanted all elements of the Catholic Church to be removed. They wanted a simpler, purer Church. Elizabeth I's compromise settlement, which blended elements of the Protestant and Catholic Churches, was not enough for them.

They did not act as one religious movement; rather they were divided into Moderates, Presbyterians and Separatists, based on their beliefs.

- Although not completely satisfied, the Moderates accepted Elizabeth I's changes and took positions in her new Church. They aimed to make small changes once they were in position, such as making priests wear simple robes.
- The Presbyterians wanted to change Elizabeth I's Church but in particular wanted to remove the bishops and, in their place, put councils of local, elected elders.
- The Separatists were more extreme than both the Presbyterians and the Moderates. They wanted to get rid of Elizabeth I's national Church completely and allow each parish to decide its own direction. Their numbers were actually quite small.

In general, the Puritans agreed that it was in their best interests not to push for Elizabeth I's removal from the throne. Despite their dislike of her religious changes, she was a better choice of queen than her Catholic cousin, Mary Stuart, who was next in line to the throne, as they knew that the latter would not tolerate any diversion from the Catholic faith.

The vestments controversy

In 1565, Elizabeth I began her attack on those who would not conform to her Religious Settlement. Matthew Parker, appointed by Elizabeth I as Archbishop of Canterbury, issued a Book of Advertisements which instructed clergy to wear a surplice and cope (cape). Some, such as Thomas Sampson and Lawrence Humphries, both **Marian exiles**, refused to conform to the instructions. They felt that the garments were too similar to Catholic robes and made them stand out as special from the laity, something which they believed Christ had abolished. Elizabeth I

SOURCE B

'whether he will more edify the church of Christ by regarding the use of habits for the sake of order and decency, as a matter of indifference' than by leaving the church altogether and allowing it 'to be occupied hereafter if not by the evident wolves, at least by ill qualified and evil ministers'.

Bullinger, a moderate Puritan, writing about how the non-conformist actions of other Puritans were a threat to the future of Protestantism and the dangers of questioning the authority of the Queen.

herself became directly involved in an attempt to force such people to conform.

Despite her best efforts and threats of punishments, some priests continued not to conform.

The threat from inside Parliament

The threat to Elizabeth I from inside Parliament was considered far more serious than those from outside, such as the vestments controversy. Thomas Cartwright, Professor of Divinity at Cambridge, criticised the organisation of Elizabeth I's Church. Although he lost his professorship as a result, his ideas were picked up by William Strickland, who introduced a Bill into Parliament wanting to reform the structure and leadership of the Church. Strickland was arrested.

Three Bills on reforming the structure of the Church were rejected by Parliament, which provoked an **admonition** to Parliament by Thomas Wilcox supported by John Field and Thomas Cartwright. Importantly, these men had political support from the Earls of Huntingdon, Leicester, Warwick and Bedford. They did not want the Queen as Supreme Governor but wanted equal ministers and a group of elders to run the Church. Elizabeth I made it quite clear she did not want matters of religion to be discussed in Parliament and used her right of prerogative to forbid any discussion. Field and Wilcox were imprisoned and Cartwright fled to the Continent.

Fact file

Prophesyings were meetings of clergy that involved prayer, instruction on preaching and the Bible. Puritans believed that they were essential to increase the number of good-quality preachers. Elizabeth felt they were unnecessary.

SOURCE C

Clergy should not desert our churches for the sake of a few ceremonies and those not unlawful in themselves, especially since the pure doctrine of the Gospel remained in all its integrity and freedom.

Edmund Grindal, a moderate Puritan, who became Archbishop of Canterbury.

SOURCE D

The Admonition full of 'unreasonableness and unseasonableness has hindered much good, and done much hurt'.

Thomas Norton, a moderate Puritan, tried to introduce Bills in Parliament to make small changes from within the established Church.

SOURCE E

Prophesying is the cause of… great numbers of our people, specially the vulgar sort… are brought to idleness and… become… divided among themselves into a variety of dangerous opinions, not only in towns and parishes but even in some families, and thereby encouraged to… break the law… and common order, offending all our quiet subjects that desire to serve God according to the uniform orders established in the church, the result is too dangerous to be suffered.

Extract from the Queen's letter to the bishops, ordering the suppression of prophesying, 1577 (adapted).

ACTIVITIES

1. Why did Elizabeth I rule that clergy should wear the dress of the traditional Catholic Church when her Church was clearly Protestant in nature?

2. According to Source A, why was Elizabeth I so determined that all clergy should obey this dress rule?

3. a. Look at Source B. According to Bullinger what danger did non-conformists pose to the future of the Church?

   b. Source B suggests why Elizabeth I allowed moderate Puritans who did not totally agree with her new Church to take up positions within it. What reason is suggested?

4. Look at Source C. Elizabeth I would have agreed with Edmund Grindal's judgement of her Religious Settlement. Explain his judgement.

5. Look at Source D. How did moderate Puritans, like Thomas Norton, feel about the admonition to Parliament?

6. According to Source E, why was Elizabeth I so against prophesying? What were the underlying issues?

7. Look at the attribution of Source E. How does the timing of this source affect its content?

GradeStudio

You have now completed this unit of work, which has focused on the religious changes made by Elizabeth I and the challenges she encountered as a result of her religious faith. You have also been given some revision tips and practised answering questions that will help you prepare for your examination.

Below is a typical examination question on Elizabethan England.

> Elizabeth's government dealt with religious problems with great success. How far do you agree with this statement? **[8 marks]**

Examiner's tips

- Use the mark allocation as a guide to how many points you should make, how long you should take answering the question and roughly how long your answer should be.
- Read the question carefully to identify the actual issue you will be evaluating. Do not write everything you know about this topic.
- Do not make generalised statements. Be clear, with specific examples.
- Perhaps begin with all the evidence for one case, then present evidence for the other. This helps you to ensure that you present a balanced view.
- When you have presented both sides, you must conclude by making a judgement. It must overview the evidence you have based it on.

Fact file

In your GCSE examination, your knowledge and understanding of a topic will be tested by questions requiring you to investigate an issue the examiner has identified for you. A high-level historical skill that will be asked of you is to evaluate an issue. This is usually asked in the form of 'How successful was…', 'How far did…' questions. This requires you to present relevant evidence from your own knowledge and understanding of a topic, then make a sound and reasoned judgement based on that evidence.

Before you write your answer, below are two things to help you start on the right lines.

Firstly, look at the simplified mark scheme. This should help you write your answer in a way which will allow you to get the full eight marks.

Simplified mark scheme

Level	Description of answer	Mark
Level 0	No evidence submitted or response does not address the question	0
Level 1	General assertions	1–2
Level 2	Identifies or describes specific examples of success or failure	2–3
Level 3	Identifies or describes specific examples of success and failure	4
Level 4	Explains specific examples of success or failure	5–6
Level 5	Explains specific examples of success and failure	6–7
Level 6	As for Level 5 but in addition explains a reason why her policies were more a success/failure	8

Secondly, look at the sample students' answers below – noting especially the examiner's comments.

Candidate 1's answer

Elizabeth I's religious policies were successful. The major changes were made through the Act of Settlement, the Act of Uniformity and the Royal Injunctions. The Catholics were pleased as their priests were encouraged to wear elaborate robes and kneeling at the altar was not forbidden. Puritans were pleased because churches had to be decorated simply and every church had to have an English Bible. The changes Elizabeth I made and the Church she made are the basis of the Church of England today.

Examiner's comment

This candidate has reached Level 3. The answer identifies and describes specific examples of successes. It describes how the Catholics were happy with certain policies and the Protestants with others. It does not explain how Catholics and Protestants felt and so the top mark scored can only be 4. In order to reach Level 4 the candidate could have mentioned the different groups within the Puritans and how they each reacted to the religious changes. They could have mentioned how angry the Separatists were with the changes because they were not extreme enough, or how unhappy the Catholics were that Elizabeth I had made herself Supreme Governor of the Church in England rather than the Pope.

To secure a Level 6 answer the candidate needed to explain all the dissatisfaction and satisfaction and use this to make a judgement on how successful the religious changes were. Look at Candidate 2's example answer below:

Candidate 2's answer

Generally the population were pleased that there was a settled period with regard to religion after the huge changes made by King Edward VI and Queen Mary I. The Catholics were not persecuted but rather Elizabeth I followed a policy of continuity. She believed that the more the new Church resembled the old Church the easier Catholics would find it to conform. Despite the fact they did not like Elizabeth I taking the title of Supreme Governor of the Church in England, the Pope at the time gave them little guidance on how to act. Many Catholics and Puritans took up positions within Elizabeth I's Church. They felt the true meaning of the Bible was still evident in the new religion and they could make small changes from within once they had taken up their new positions. Some Puritans, such as the Separatists, were determined not to accept Elizabeth I's new Church. However, they were a small group. The Puritans, although they disagreed with many of Elizabeth I's policies, knew if they did not accept her as queen the next in line was the Catholic Mary Stuart.

In conclusion, the changes that Elizabeth I made during her reign to religion form the basis of the Church of England today and so there must have been great strengths in them. There were few religious revolts and those that did happen, like the Babington Plot were dealt with swiftly.

Chapter 3

Was Elizabethan society a divided society?

Before

During the reign of Henry VIII, the situation of the poor became worse. Henry VIII's Reformation of the Church meant that monasteries were closed. One of the monasteries' tasks had been to give charity to the poor. Also, as the Tudor period advanced so did changes in agriculture and with it came enclosure. Enclosure of the countryside meant that many lost their jobs and their homes. In addition, foreign wars throughout the reigns of Henry VIII, Edward VI and Mary I meant that taxation was high and in order to solve their financial problems they issued coins that were lighter than the value of the metal they represented. This is called debasement of coinage. Prices rose and so Elizabeth I inherited huge debt, a debased economy and high inflation. The level of poverty on her accession continued to increase.

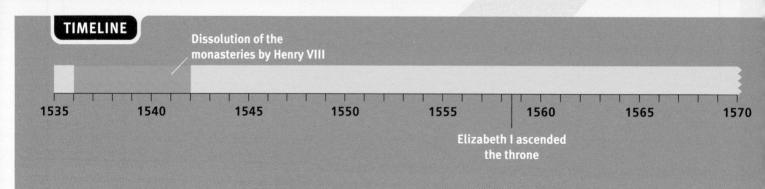

TIMELINE

Dissolution of the monasteries by Henry VIII

1535   1540   1545   1550   1555   1560   1565   1570

Elizabeth I ascended the throne

After

Elizabeth I's reign saw the development of an enlightened attitude towards the care of the poor. Central government began to accept responsibility for providing a minimum level of subsistence and local areas began to take responsibility for finding work for the poor rather than simply punishing them for their situation. Even the poor harvests of the 1590s and the consequent famine did not produce riots and rebellions. Elizabeth I's laws on poverty were some of the most successful achievements of her reign and did in fact remain in force for over 250 years.

ACTIVITY

Due to an injury to your arm you have been working too slowly so your employer has sacked you. As your wife is just about to give birth and your two children are still too young to work, you need to think about how you are going to get through the winter.

The cartoon illustrates everything that people have told you about the current help for the poor. What are you thinking? How will you manage?

Think about:

- Why so many people are poor.
- Why you will have to convince people that you are genuinely poor.
- The attitudes of the rich generally towards the poor.
- How you might be treated by the authorities.
- What methods of charity are there and why they are no longer an option.
- What help could you get from the queen directly.

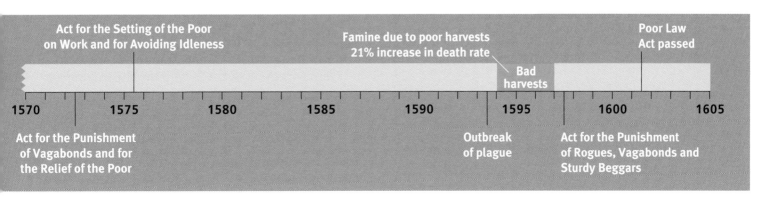

Act for the Setting of the Poor on Work and for Avoiding Idleness

Famine due to poor harvests 21% increase in death rate

Poor Law Act passed

Bad harvests

1570 1575 1580 1585 1590 1595 1600 1605

Act for the Punishment of Vagabonds and for the Relief of the Poor

Outbreak of plague

Act for the Punishment of Rogues, Vagabonds and Sturdy Beggars

3.1 What was the nature of vagabondage and poverty?

LEARNING OBJECTIVES

In this lesson you will:

- understand the nature of vagabondage in the Elizabethan era
- practise using source comprehension skills.

KEY WORDS

Poverty – *the state of being poor.*
Vagabond – *an idle poor person also known as a sturdy beggar.*

The nature of Elizabethan poverty

During the Elizabethan era, society had a very clear structure. Gentlemen were at the top of the structure. They included dukes, earls, knights and squires. The next level of society were the citizens. These were freemen who lived in the cities. Next came the yeomen, who owned a small amount of land. Lastly, at the very bottom of the structure, were day labourers, farm workers, shopkeepers and craftsmen. It was from this bottom layer of society that the poor came.

During the Elizabethan era there were many reasons why people became poor. A family could become poor as the result of the loss of the main wage earner. As there were no old-age pensions, old age often meant people were thrown

Fact file

Types of Elizabethan undeserving poor

- Ruffler – pretended to be an out-of-work ex-soldier but really robbed passers-by.
- Rogueman/angler – used a long stick to rob clothes that were out to dry.
- Counterfeit crank – pretended to be too ill to work by having a fit by swallowing soap.
- Clapper dudgeon – pretended to be too ill to work by putting arsenic on their skin so it bled.
- Prigger of palfreys – pretended to be a beggar but actually stole horses.
- Tom O'Bedlam – pretended to be mad so they did not have to work.

SOURCE A

Lame beggars, a maundering (travelling) beggar and a gallant beggar pictured in an Elizabethan woodcut.

SOURCE B

With us the poor is commonly divided into three sorts, so that some are poor by impotency (not through their own fault), as the fatherless child, the aged, blind, lame, and the diseased person that is judged to be incurable; the second are poor by casualty, as the wounded soldier, the decayed householder, and the sick person visited with grievous and painful disease; the third consisteth of thriftless poor, as the rioter that hath consumed all, the vagabond that will abide nowhere, but runneth up and down from place to place, and finally the rogue and the strumpet (prostitute).

From a description of England by William Harrison in 1577, describing the structure of Elizabethan society.

11 Wylson Thomas	Thomas Wylson, of 30 yeris, a basket maker, & Katherin, his wyf, of 25 yeres, who make buttons; 2 daughters, the eldest 5 yeris. They have dwelt here ever. [Hable to work].	Balistons house. Indeferent. No almes. 2 spare.	St. Peter of South gate
12 Coke Myhell	Myhell Coke, of 40 yeris, a laborer, & … his wyf, of 50 yeris. They lyve together, & have dwelt here above 3 yeris. [hable].	Edward Paulins house. No almes. Indeferent.	St. Peter of South gate
13 Fyld Nycholas	Nycholas Fyld of 30 yeris, laborer, sometym a paynter, & Rose, his wyfe, of 30 ycris, who spyn white warpe; & 2 sons, the eldest 6 yeris. They kepe together & worke, & have dwelt here ever. [hable]	Paulins house, Veri Pore. No almes.	St. Peter of South gate
14 Soule John	Also John Soule of 40 yeris, laborer, & Alice, his wyfe, of 60 yeris, who spyn white warpe, & no child, & they lyve together, & dwelt her ever. [hable][gon to St. Stevens].	Indeferent. No almes. [Veri Pore].	St. Peter of South gate
15 Bundi John	John Bundi of 60 yeris, laborer & Elizabeth, his wyfe of 40 yeris, who spyn hir owne woolle; & 1 son of 12 yeris that is ydle & a daughter of 12 yeris that spyn woolle. They dwell together, & have dwelt her ever.	Paulins house. Veri pore. Skouldes.	St. Peter of South gate

Part of the City of Norwich survey, 1570.

into **poverty**. This was also the case with illness or disability. When harvests were bad and when there were slumps in industry, the price of goods went up, the price of wages went down, and people were thrown out of work. These people who became poor through no fault of their own became known as the 'deserving poor'.

There were others who claimed to be poor but in fact were pretending to be poor so they could live off charity rather than work for a living. These people became known as the 'idle poor' or the 'undeserving poor'. They were also called **vagabonds** or sturdy beggars. They caused huge worries for the authorities as there was no organised police force to control them.

In 1570 Norwich City Council conducted a census of its urban population. Source C shows a sample of the 800 residents who were surveyed. Of the total: 17 per cent came from broken homes, 25 per cent suffered from illness or old age, 45 per cent were unable to work, 8 per cent were from large families, 17 per cent were unemployed. The total exceeds 100 per cent because some people were in two or more categories.

ACTIVITIES

1 Look at Source A carefully. Describe all of the beggars in the picture, highlighting the differences between them.
2 According to William Harrison in Source B, who were the poor?
3 According to Sources A and B, why was the issue of poverty complicated and how did the Elizabethans attempt to simplify it?
4 a According to Source C, was the issue of poverty a problem for Norwich?
   b How useful is this census for indicating the extent of poverty in the rest of England?

HISTORY DETECTIVE

Find out what a census is. When did they begin? What can historians use them for? For times when census information was not collected, what other sources of this sort of information can we use? Look on the Internet or in an encyclopedia to find out.

3.2 What were the long-term and short-term causes of an increase in Elizabethan poverty?

LEARNING OBJECTIVES

In this lesson you will:

- learn about the long-term and short-term causes of the increase in poverty in Elizabethan England
- practise cross-referencing sources.

GETTING STARTED

Discuss with a partner the reasons why people become poor today. Could it be the loss of a job, redundancy, disability, illness, the development of technology, lack of inclination to work? What help is there for people who find themselves in this situation? Do you know anyone this has happened to? What about in the past? Do you think that people became poor for the same reasons? What help was available for them?

KEY WORDS

Birth rate – *number of births in a population.*

Common field systems – *a system of dividing up the land in a parish for agricultural use begun in Anglo Saxon times.*

Common land – *land owned by one person but others have the right to graze livestock, collect berries for food or gather wood for fuel, etc.*

Death rate – *number of deaths in a population.*

Enclosure – *hedges, walls or ditches used to enclose land into small fields and placed under private ownership.*

Inflation – *an increase in the amount of currency being used but matched or outpaced by the unavailability of goods which leads to higher prices. Therefore, there is no benefit or real meaning to the rising level of wages.*

Short-term causes of an increase in poverty

Throughout the reign of Elizabeth I, the population of England grew from approximately 3 million to 4 million. The largest areas of population growth were in the south-east and the Midlands. Apart from a short outbreak of the plague and typhus, there were fewer epidemic diseases during this period so the **death rate** decreased. At the same time, the **birth rate** was increasing as the age of marriage became lower and women had children younger as a result of times of prosperity. This meant more people being born who were living longer. The result was a growth in population.

- Population growth meant more people which meant more competition for jobs and employers could lower wages.

- Between 1594 and 1597 there were four bad harvests. The demand for food outstripped supply. As there was so little food available, those that had food to sell could demand high prices which many people were unable to afford (see Source A).

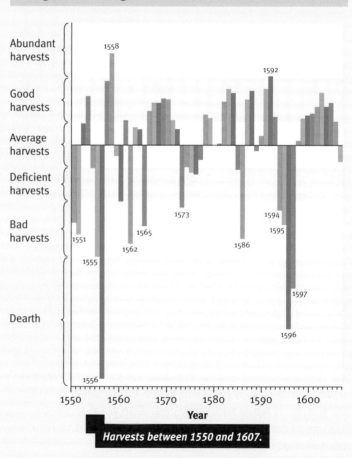

Harvests between 1550 and 1607.

- Expensive wars were being fought for which the government demanded high taxes. War affected industry as trade with other countries was curtailed. This particularly affected the woollen industry with many people losing jobs.

Families struggled to manage with falling incomes and the rising cost of living. In order to survive, they turned to charity. Increases in the cost of looking after the poor suggest there was a significant increase in their numbers.

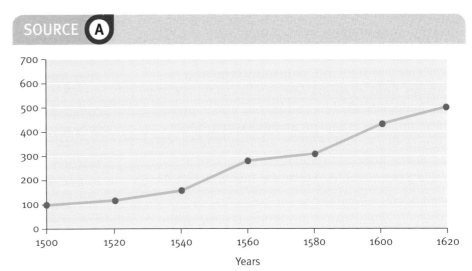

SOURCE A

Rising prices during the Elizabethan period.

Long-term causes of the increase in poverty

Although there were many short-term causes of the increase in the number of poor during the reign of Elizabeth I, historians argue that some of the causes were more long term, due to events that had happened before Elizabeth I became queen.

Closure of monasteries

When Elizabeth I's father, Henry VIII, broke with the Roman Catholic Church, it not only gave him control over spiritual matters in England but also gave him control over the physical assets of the Church. As a result, Henry VIII closed all the monasteries and the nunneries under the advice of his main advisers in order to sell the buildings and the contents to fund expensive wars. Therefore, there was less support for the poor in need. Source B lists the jobs that a monk in the St Augustine order might have carried out to support the local community.

SOURCE B

Jobs to be done by monks
1 Copying books
2 Looking after the poor and old
3 Nursing the sick and crippled
4 Looking after travellers by giving them a bed and food
5 Praying to God and helping everyone get to heaven
6 Teaching boys
7 Giving generously to those in need and visiting those who are ill

Extracts from the Rule of St Augustine, a guide to religious life.

HISTORY DETECTIVE

Is there a monastery or abbey near where you live that was closed down by Henry VIII? Find out more about what happened.

Fountains Abbey was closed down by Henry VIII in 1539. For 400 years it had served as an important part of the community in North Yorkshire.

Enclosure

Throughout the Tudor period there were changes in the way agricultural land was used. To improve the productivity of the land, **common land** and **common field systems** were enclosed with stone walls, hedges or ditches and placed under private ownership. This is known as **enclosure**. Some landlords also hoped through enclosure to increase rents. Some hoped to reduce their workforce, changing from arable to pastoral farming which required fewer workers.

The effects of enclosure on the rural population were thought to be many. It caused unemployment, it also caused hunger and deprivation. Villagers no longer had access to common land to graze animals and to collect berries and firewood (see Source B). Amalgamation of farms reduced the number of homes available. The increase in pastoral farming increased the impact of bad harvests. However, it is important to bear in mind that between 1500 and 1600 only 2 per cent of land was enclosed.

SOURCE C

Noblemen and gentlemen enclose all into pasture. They thrown down houses. The poor people be forced out, or else by wrongs and injuries they be compelled to sell all. By one means or another they must depart away, poor wretched souls. Men, women, fatherless children, widows, woeful mothers with their young babes – away they trudge. All their household stuff, which is worth very little, they be forced to sell for hardly anything. And when they have wandered about til they have spent that, what can they do but steal, and then be hanged, or go about begging?

Sir Thomas More, *Utopia*, 1516.

HISTORY DETECTIVE

Find out more about Sir Thomas More, what he believed in, why he was executed and why he was canonised (made a saint) in 1937.

Harvest in Tudor times.

GradeStudio

Analysis of sources

1 How far do Sources B and C agree or disagree on the reasons for an increase in the number of poor during Elizabeth I's reign?

In order to write a high-level answer to this question, you need to incorporate the following:

- Describe how Source B gives the reason for an increase in the number of the poor as the dissolution of the monasteries (i.e. the assistance the monks gave to the poor disappeared with the monastery). A long-term cause.

- Highlight the differences in the reason the sources give by describing how Source C gives enclosure as the main reason. Less labour was needed in pastoral farming and the vital common land was disappearing. A short-term cause.

- Explain how the two sources agree by considering how the two impacted upon each other. Those left without work due to enclosure could no longer get short-term help until they found work. Their situation then became worse and they dropped into long-term poverty.

Examiner's tip

On the surface, sources will often appear to agree/disagree. Look deeper than the surface of the source. If you analyse the link between the content of the sources or the tone and attitude they take towards an issue, you may find more ways in which they agree or disagree.

2 Source A gives another reason for an increase in the numbers of the poor during the reign of Elizabeth I. How far does it agree with Sources B and C?

Use the same strategy outlined above to answer this question successfully.

BRAIN BOOST

A good way to revise is to use sticky notes. Put basic facts on one set of notes, such as the causes of an increase in poverty throughout the Elizabethan period. You could use two different colours to differentiate between the long-term and short-term causes of the increase in the numbers of poor. Stick the notes in places in the house that you visit often, like the fridge or the bathroom mirror. Look at them each time you visit that place. They will be a regular reminder of the facts you need to know. You can mix the long-term and short-term causes up and move them around, separating them into long-term and short-term. This is almost like creating an essay plan. Later during your revision, stick those facts that you can remember on one wall and those you cannot remember on another wall. This will help you to focus on revising the topics you find difficult and should make revision more fun!

3.3 Why were Elizabeth I and her government so concerned with poverty?

In this lesson you will:

- understand why Elizabeth I and her government were so concerned about the poor
- practise using source comprehension skills.

KEY WORDS

Alms – charity, usually in the form of money.

Licentiousness – pursuing desires aggressively and selfishly, unchecked by morality.

Why were Elizabeth I and her government so concerned about poverty?

The issue of poverty troubled all of the monarchs of the Tudor period. Henry VIII, Elizabeth I's father, had granted licences to beggars. Only those with a licence were allowed to beg. Those without were punished severely. Edward VI, Elizabeth I's brother, took a firmer position on the poor. He declared that he would have the tongues of those considered to be idle poor branded and they were given as slaves to the rich for two years. The children of beggars were taken away from them and forced to become domestic servants. How a king or queen dealt with the poor was a signal to their people about what was acceptable and what was not.

The very structure of Elizabethan society meant that poverty was an accepted part of the fabric of life. The poor kept the rich in riches by toiling for them and paying taxes. The charity of the rich to the poor was also an accepted part of life. Many of the rich felt that it was their moral obligation to help the poor and for some it allowed them to feel, and be seen to be, superior. They often left money in their wills for those needing assistance and built rows of almshouses for the poor to live in.

The social, religious and economic conditions specific to Elizabeth I's reign very much dictated how she and her government behaved towards her poorer subjects. (See Sources A–D.)

Whilst some felt a moral obligation to help the poor the Elizabethan government feared that groups of poor could lead to a threat to law and order.

SOURCE A

Elizabeth sought to display her care for the poor by her carefully staged charity. Her almoners staff grace 5d each to 13 poor men every day at the palace gates; about £130.00 was handed out to the poor over Easter... In addition she gave an average of about £240.00 a year in casual alms to the poor, especially on progress. Perhaps one reason for the loyal crowds around her coach was that there was often money to be had.

C. Haigh, *Elizabeth I*, 1998, describing the public and well-publicised gestures of Elizabeth I.

SOURCE B

The work ethic was an essential ingredient in living a godly life, while the idle were damned since they displayed vices like shiftlessness instead of fortitude and hard work. This was particularly apparent in the vagrant poor since they were most likely to be connected with crime. On the other hand, the accumulation of wealth, according to the Protestant ethic should not be channelled into the pursuit of pleasure, which meant there was a charitable outlet for those of the poor who were considered to be deserving of it.

S. Lee, *The Reign of Elizabeth I, 1588–1603*, 2007.

Licentiousness hath grown so far as it is usual not only with common and ordinary persons travelling by the highways to carry pistols and other kinds of pieces, but that ruffians and other lewd and dissolute men… wheresoever they go ride in the highways or streets… do in secret manner go provided of such means to do mischief.

Elizabethan government, criticising authorities for the level of crime.

Sins of all sorts swarmeth.

William Lambarde, a Kent Justice of the Peace, commenting on the increase in the number of prosecutions from 33 per year 1571–75 to 70 per year 1596–1600.

Decade	Nominal wages – amount of wages received by unskilled workers	Real wages – amount of goods money will actually buy for unskilled workers
1550–59	159	75
1560–69	200	90
1570–79	200	84
1580–89	200	78
1590–99	222	71

The level of wages and what they could buy, dependent upon prices in London.

ACTIVITIES

Reason	Explanation of the reason	Which source did you use?	Evidence from the source
Public image of Elizabeth I			
Religious beliefs encouraged during the reign of Elizabeth I			
Level of crime			
Inflation and the increasing number of the poor			

1 Sources A–E give many reasons why Elizabeth I and her government were concerned by the issue of poverty. Copy and complete the above table.

2 Use the information in your completed table to answer the following:

Elizabeth I cared for her subjects greatly and they in turn cared for her. This is the main reason for her interest in the poor.

Do you agree or disagree? Explain your answer.

3.4 Get your sources sorted!

How did attitudes and policies towards the poor change during Elizabeth I's reign?

LEARNING OBJECTIVES

In this lesson you will:

- understand changing attitudes towards poverty throughout the Elizabethan period
- practise evaluating the usefulness of sources.

KEY WORDS

Evaluate – *judge.*

How do you evaluate the usefulness of a source?

As a historian, you must always be aware of how much information a source tells you. It is just as important to be aware of what the source does *not* tell you. This will enable you to make a judgement on whether a source is useful for a given topic. This is a high-level historical skill that requires you to use your source comprehension skills while testing your knowledge and understanding of the period being studied. Remember, as a general rule, no single source can ever give you all the information on a topic. At the same time, no source is useless. In some cases, the content may not be as revealing as you would like but sources often reflect opinions and beliefs of the time.

Answering 'evaluating the usefulness of a source' questions in practice

How useful is Source A on government and public attitudes towards the poor during the Elizabethan period? **[7 marks]**

SOURCE A

Procession through the streets – public humiliation

Public hanging with crowds watching – reminder this is the next punishment for them

Onlookers – show little public sympathy

Woman and child begging – highlights the different types of Elizabethan poor

Whipping him half naked – harsh punishment

Punishment of the idle poor – an Elizabethan woodcut.

Examiner's tips

Answering '**evaluating** the usefulness of a source' questions:
- Study the source carefully, ensuring that you understand its content. Also look for what it suggests or infers.
- Consider how the information in the source fits in with your knowledge and understanding of this topic. Does it reflect public opinion of the time? Does it show/suggest things that you know to be true?

- Highlight each piece of information a source gives and back it up with specific historical facts or generalise out from the source to general historical themes and ideas of the time.
- The most important part of your answer is to consider what questions are left unanswered, what gaps or inconsistencies does the source leave unfulfilled?
- Finally make a well-informed judgement on the usefulness of the source. Possibly suggest other sources it could be combined with to give it completeness.

The student has planned their answer first by making notes around the source. This is allowed during the examination but will obviously not count towards your answer. A few minutes spent planning will help you to arrange the comments you want to make into a logical order.

Read the student's answer carefully. It follows all the examiner's tips.

The source shows a member of the 'idle poor' being whipped and paraded through the street. There is a public hanging in the background as a reminder that this is the punishment if he is found begging again. The government acted harshly as they worried about the increasing number of poor and the threat to law and order. It reflects Protestant ideas about work ethic. It shows little charity given to the 'deserving' poor lady either as the people in their houses look on. In conclusion this source does not tell us how many poor were punished in this way or how successful these new punishments were. It does not suggest how the authorities decided who was a 'deserving' poor and who was an 'idle' poor, which was difficult, as poverty can lead to petty crime in order to stay alive. Perhaps combined with a source from a beggar who had no choice but to turn to petty crime, this source would be more useful.

SOURCE B

29th March 1573. At Harrow Hill in Middlesex, on the said day, John Allan, Elizabeth Taylor, Humphrey Foxe, Henry Bower and Agnes Vort, being over 14 years and having no lawful means of livelihood, were declared vagabonds. Sentenced to be flogged and burnt through the right ear.

Middlesex County Records, 1573.

GradeStudio

How useful is Source B on government and public attitudes towards the poor during the Elizabethan period?

To answer this question use the examiner's tips and refer to the student's answer about Source A. Try to annotate Source B first, then construct your answer using that information. This will ensure that you do not miss anything out but also encourage you to think about the content and whole tone of the source before you begin to write a full answer.

3.5 How did treatment of the poor change throughout the period?

LEARNING OBJECTIVES

In this lesson you will:

- learn about the changing nature of the laws passed to tackle the issue of poverty
- practise evaluating the success of these significant changes.

KEY WORDS

Conformity – *doing what is expected, in this case doing what is expected by Elizabeth I.*

Enlightened – *embraced new ideas of the age, such as sharing responsibility for the poor rather than punishing them.*

Punitive – *seen as punishments.*

How did the treatment of the poor change?

Attitudes towards poverty changed throughout the Tudor period. Charity became more and more selective and less unconditional. This was linked to religious beliefs, social understanding and, of course, the increasing numbers of poor people. There was no established police force and following the Rebellion of the Northern Earls, the threat of further unrest was great. Elizabeth I was also a great believer in **conformity** and control by the state as she had showed with regard to religion.

The government were forced into action and passed laws to deal with the whole issue of poverty. Some laws were **enlightened** and others incredibly harsh, some related to the punishment of the undeserving poor while others related to those responsible for the care of the poor. All the laws passed differentiated further between the 'idle poor' and the 'deserving poor'. The measures were largely a reaction to the conditions at that particular time, but together show a progressive attitude towards the issue of poverty throughout Elizabeth I's reign, culminating in the 1601 Poor Law Act.

GETTING STARTED

Discuss the following as a group: What makes people poor today? How are the poor cared for now by the public and the government? What help and support are the poor entitled to? Why has this help and support been put in place? If it was not there, what would be the outcome? Consider your discussion when you analyse Elizabethan laws regarding poverty. Were they supportive or **punitive**?

1572 Act for the Punishment of Vagabonds and the Relief of the Poor

All vagabonds above age 14 to be whipped and burned through the right ear

Imprisonment to be the punishment for a second offence

Persistent offenders would be executed

Children of convicted beggars were put in domestic service

A national poor law rate was established

1576 Act for the Setting of the Poor on Work and for Avoiding Idleness

Towns required to give the unemployed work

If they refused to work, placed in a local prison

Prison to be financed from a local tax, the rates

In 1563, it became law that anyone who refused to pay for the aid of the poor would face imprisonment. Fines were introduced from £2 to £20 for officials who failed to organise help for the poor.

1597 Act for the Punishment of Rogues, Vagabonds and Sturdy Beggars

All counties and cities to have local prisons

Anyone caught begging for the first time to be whipped and sent back to the parish of their birth

Persistent re-offenders to be sent to the gallows and executed

Each parish to appoint an overseer of the poor to find work for young unemployed and hand out help to the deserving poor

1601 Poor Law Act

Each parish to look after their own poor

Church wardens to collect the poor rate

Church wardens to help the poor who were poor through no fault of their own

Idle poor or sturdy beggars to be whipped and made to work or sent to prison

Beggars from elsewhere to be whipped and sent home

Those who could not work were to be looked after in their own homes using money from the poor rate

Orphans to be fostered or sent to work as apprentices

GradeStudio

Recall and select knowledge

How did the laws passed on poverty and vagabondage during the reign of Elizabeth I illustrate a change in attitude towards the issue of poverty?

Look at the terms of the Acts carefully. Fill in each of the columns of the table below. Use this table as a plan and write an answer to the question. A Level 3 response would comment on which aspects of the Acts were increasingly harsh yet included enlightened attitudes towards the poor. It would then explain what change in attitude is illustrated.

Examiner's tip

When given the terms of an Act, look closely at the date and use your historical knowledge and understanding to contextualise it. If you do this, it helps you to better understand the nature of the terms and the attitude of the time that the Act illustrates, which you'll need to do to achieve a Level 3 answer.

Date of the Act?	Who did it affect?	Which parts of the Act showed a harsh attitude to the poor?	Which parts of the Act were enlightened?	What changes in attitude did it show?

3.6 How effective were Elizabethan policies on poverty?

LEARNING OBJECTIVES

In this lesson you will:

- evaluate the effectiveness of Elizabethan laws on poverty
- practise analysing different interpretations of the effects of significant changes in the past.

KEY WORDS

Infrastructure – *the basic organisation needed.*

Interpretation – *the meaning of something to someone; in particular, their view of an event.*

Legislation – *laws passed.*

How effective were Elizabethan policies on vagabondage and poverty?

There was a flurry of **legislation** regarding the poor during the Elizabethan period. This was often in response to immediate circumstances. The Northern Rebellion of 1569 stimulated the 1572 and 1576 Acts, and the poor harvests of the 1590s provoked the 1597 Act. The terms of these Acts ensured that a national poor rate to pay for the upkeep of the poor was established and an overseer was appointed to organise support for the poor.

Throughout the periods of food shortages, there were no major disturbances. By the end of Elizabeth I's reign, the government had accepted their social responsibility to support the poor. Measures had been put in place to deal with the idle poor, making an example of them and thereby discouraging others to follow suit. An **infrastructure** of support for the deserving poor had been gradually put in place throughout the period. Indeed, the Poor Law of 1601 remained in force for 250 years, which must be some judgement on the success of Elizabethan measures on poverty.

SOURCE

... the Queen is but a woman, and ruled by noblemen, and the noblemen and gentlemen are all one, and the gentlemen and farmers will hold together so that the poor can get nothing – we shall never have a merry world while the Queen liveth.

An Essex labourer, 1591.

$$\text{Northern Rebellion} + \text{Poor harvests} = \text{Poor Law 1601}$$

SOURCE C

The problem of poverty appeared to have been contained by the end of the Tudor period because the economic conditions which had contributed to it were being alleviated. By the last years of Elizabeth's reign the demand for food was being recognised as a possible source for profit, while the cloth trade had been disrupted by the wars with Spain. Both of these slowed – and then reversed – the swing from arable to pastoral agriculture. The move back to food production at the end of the sixteenth century therefore meant an increase in demand for employment, which began to check the problem of vagrancy. The economy and society were, by the end of Elizabeth's reign, beginning to move into closer harmony with each other, irrespective of government policy.

S. Lee, *The Reign of Elizabeth I, 1558–1603*, 2007.

SOURCE

In normal circumstances both poverty and vagrancy were fairly well contained, and to say that either created a dangerous national situation would be to strain the evidence.

J. Pound, *Poverty and Vagrancy in Tudor England*, 1978.

GradeStudio

Study Sources A–C. How far do these sources prove that Elizabethan governments successfully dealt with the problem of poverty? Use the sources and your knowledge to explain your answer. **(7 marks)**

To answer the question successfully you need to:

1 Read the sources carefully and use the information they contain in your answer.

2 Use your contextual historical knowledge to argue your answer.

3 Explain ways in which the government succeeded and did not succeed.

Examiner's tips

Often, when modern historians **interpret** the effects of a significant event or change, they have the benefit of hindsight. This means they can assess the effects based on events that followed and make connections between an event or change and others that came after it that were similar. It also means they may have access to information that commentators at the time did not. Therefore, always take this into account when considering why their interpretation may be different than interpretations made at the time.

Aims of the Elizabethan Acts on poverty	Explain ways government was failing to deal with/understand the problem of poverty	Explain ways government was succeeding/beginning to succeed in dealing with/understanding the problem of poverty
Central government accepted responsibility for the minimum level of subsistence for the poor		
To prevent major outbreaks of unrest among the poor during periods of unrest		
To deal with the increasing number of idle poor and vagrants		
To deal with the increasing number of deserving poor who could not find work		
To ensure that the rich took responsibility for financing the care of the poor		

An engraving of a beggar family in Tudor times. Was the engraver sympathetic to the plight of the poor?

3.7 Why was the Elizabethan period a great period for the development of culture?

LEARNING OBJECTIVES

In this lesson you will:

- learn about why the Elizabethan period was one of great cultural change
- practise using source comprehension skills.

KEY WORDS

Elite culture – *what the rich did in their leisure time, such as hunting, fishing and reading/writing poetry.*

Popular culture – *what the general public did in their leisure time, such as bear-baiting and cock-fighting.*

Renaissance – *a rebirth or revival of, for example, culture, skills or learning, that had been forgotten or previously ignored. Begun in Italy in the 15th century.*

GETTING STARTED

What do you think of when we talk about British culture? What images, sights, sounds and words come into your head when you think about what makes Britain 'British'? Are there differences around the country? Are there different cultures within a larger culture? What has influenced the development of today's British culture? Discuss this as a group. Compare your conclusions with the Elizabethan era that you will investigate below.

The development of Elizabethan culture

The Tudor period was one of great cultural change but there was a particularly significant development of culture during the reign of Elizabeth I. **Popular culture** grew where people enjoyed watching punishments such as executions and taunting people in the stocks. They also enjoyed bear-baiting, fairs and markets and watching processions, such as the Queen's progresses. **Elite culture** grew also but this was the preserve of the select few. Architecture developed its own unique style, music was enhanced by composers such as Thomas Tallis and manners and social refinement were developed at the court of Elizabeth I. The growth of elite culture and popular culture overlapped with a flurry of plays, poetry, ballads and the building of theatres during Elizabeth I's reign.

Elizabeth I, like her father, was a huge patron of the arts. In part, this was an attempt to raise her profile with her people.

SOURCE A

*Ring out your bells!
What should you do else?
Strike up your drums for joy;
The noblest Queen
That ever was seen
In England doth reign this day!*

Unofficial propaganda – a popular ballad printed in 1600 and reprinted in 1601 and 1602.

SOURCE B

The growth of printing presses began during the period of 'new learning' of the **Renaissance**. By 1603, the majority of the yeomanry and gentlemen were literate. Cheap books were sold by pedlars, while gentlemen filled their libraries with expensive books.

Jesus College, Oxford, founded in 1571. The number of schools and higher education establishments increased.

Henry VIII's split with the Catholic Church and the dissolution of the monasteries meant that Catholic ritual and superstition was replaced by rationalism.

ACTIVITIES

1 Look at Source A carefully.
- What is the ballad about?
- Who would the audience have been?
- Why would the ballad have been produced?

2 Look at Source B. The Renaissance brought with it 'new learning'.
- How was this new learning spread?
- Who was the audience for the new learning?

3 Look at Source C. According to this source, what else stimulated the development of Elizabethan culture?

4 According to Source D, how did the Reformation impact on the development of Elizabethan culture?

5 Think about all your answers to the above questions. To what extent was Elizabeth I's reign 'a golden age' for English culture?

TAKING IT FURTHER

Elizabethan culture covers art, theatre, poetry, music and architecture. List as many composers, playwrights, poets, architects, famous paintings, buildings and plays from the period as you can. If you think carefully, you will be able to name some of these without any research, particularly famous playwrights of the age and some of the Tudor black and white buildings that featured heavily in this period. When you have exhausted those you know already, search on the Internet, in encyclopedias and in information leaflets from organisations like the National Trust or English Heritage.

3.8 How did society and the government react towards plays and theatre-going?

LEARNING OBJECTIVES

In this lesson you will:
- investigate reactions of the people and the government towards plays and theatre-going
- practise using source comprehension skills.

KEY WORDS

Groundlings – *those who paid a penny to stand and watch the play from the pit.*
Playwright – *a writer of plays.*
Vagrant – *sturdy beggar, idle poor.*

Society reaction

The development of elite culture and popular culture overlapped with the growth of drama plays. Strolling plays and players had been popular for centuries. Entertainers performed in inn yards and open spaces where they could attract a crowd. The Elizabethan period saw the building of purpose-built, open-air theatres in London. The first named theatre was built in Shoreditch in 1576 by James Burbage. It was called the Theatre. Another theatre, the Curtain Theatre was built nearby in 1577 and soon after others were built across the Thames or outside the city walls, such as the Globe Theatre and the Fortune Theatre. By 1600 there were eight theatres operating in London. The theatres were round and had no roofs. The stage jutted out. Theatre-goers could stand near the stage in 'the pit' for one penny (such people were known as **groundlings**), or pay more to sit in the covered seats in the galleries. Low ticket prices meant that many Londoners could regularly go to the theatre. Theatres such as the Globe were also bear pits, brothels and gambling houses.

An Elizabethan trip to the theatre was not as ordered as it is today. People moved around continually to buy food and drink and, as some people were not literate enough to understand the play, they would talk all the way through it. If the audience did not like the play, they would throw rotten fruit at the actors. (The actors were all male with boys acting in the female roles.)

Many **playwrights** became famous at this time, such as Christopher Marlowe, Thomas Kyd and Ben Jonson. However, the Elizabethan period is commonly referred to as the 'age of Shakespeare'.

SOURCE A

*They are the ordinary places for **vagrants**, thieves, coney-catchers and other idle and dangerous persons to meet together to the great displeasure of Almighty God and the hurt and annoyance of Her Majesty's people. They maintain idleness and persons who have no vocation (job), and draw apprentices and servants from their other work and all sorts of people away from sermons and other Christian exercises.*

In times of sickness many walk abroad and amuse themselves by hearing a play, whereby others are infected.

The Lord Mayor and Alderman, complaining about theatres in 1597.

William Shakespeare was a prolific playwright meeting the ever increasing demand for new plays. Many of his plays were watched by Elizabeth I.

Government reaction

Elizabeth I was worried that the theatre could be used to spread propaganda. One theatre could house an audience of 3000; the population of London at the time was 200,000 making this 1.5 per cent of the population in one place at one time. Elizabeth feared that the audience would hear religious or political messages against the state and be encouraged to rebel leading to a collapse of law and order. Of particular concern to the government were the theatres springing up outside the city walls where they had less control. They also feared that many people close together would cause the spread of infectious diseases.

In order to combat this threat Elizabeth introduced censorship laws and systems in 1572. The Lord Chamberlain was put in charge of the censorship of plays and granting licences to organised acting companies. All play scripts had to be submitted before they were performed to the Lord Chamberlain's assistant, the Master of the Revels. He would check there was no inappropriate language used, no religious or political messages, and no inappropriate references made to the royal family. Punishments for breaking any of the censorship laws or performing without a licence could be mutilation, torture or imprisonment.

Elizabeth's concerns about the gatherings of people in the theatres and their potential to spread messages of propaganda turned out in some cases to be real. Thomas Nashe and Ben Jonson's play *The Isle of Dogs* was suppressed by the Master of the Revels. It was never printed as the authorities felt it was an attack on Elizabeth's courtiers. The playwrights were imprisoned and the Privy Council banned all plays in London for the rest of the year.

The leading actors of Shakespeare's play *Richard II* were interrogated. The play had been commissioned by the Earl of Essex who was attempting to rebel against the Queen (see page 23). The play *Sir Thomas More* by Anthony Mundy and others was also suppressed and never granted a licence. It was censored by the Master of the Revels, Edmund Tilney, in the 1590s. His marks and deletions can be seen on an original of the manuscript. Tilney deleted anything that would incite the people to unrest as the text was understanding of the plight of the poor.

(see page 23)

SOURCE B

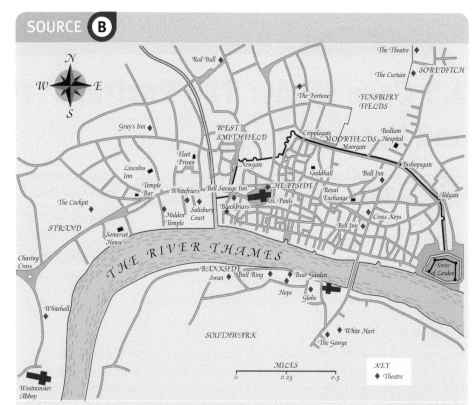

Location of Elizabethan theatres in London, 1596. The government banned theatres within the city walls. In 1593, 1603 and 1608, all places of Elizabethan entertainment including the Globe Theatre were closed to prevent the spread of the plague.

ACTIVITY

Complete the speech bubbles for each of the characters. They should be describing how they feel about plays and theatre-going and explain why they feel the way they do. In order to complete the task, you will need to use the sources and think about:
- Elizabethan views on social order.
- Elizabeth I's patronage of the arts to raise her profile with the people.
- Elizabethan attitude towards the 'idle' poor.
- The spread of ideas through popular culture e.g. reference to the economic crisis of the time in plays.
- The overlap between elite and popular culture.
- Elizabethan ideas on public health and the spread of disease.

Vagrant

Poorer working man

The Lord Mayor

Queen Elizabeth I

SOURCE C

The ox hath therefore stretch'd his yoke in vain,
The ploughman lost his sweat, and the green corn
Hath rotted ere his youth attain'd a beard.

Titania speaking in *A Midsummer's Nights Dream* by Shakespeare.
This quote is thought to be a reference to the bad harvests in the years 1595–96.

3.9 Case study: The Puritans' reaction to plays and theatre-going

LEARNING OBJECTIVES

In this lesson you will:

- investigate reactions of the Puritans towards plays and theatre-going
- practise using source comprehension skills.

KEY WORDS

Popish – *as the leader of the Catholic Church, the Pope, would like it.*

Sacrilegious – *against the will of God.*

Salvation – *saving of the soul.*

A place of sin

The violence and lawlessness of the theatre was reason enough for complaint. However, the Church felt that the theatre and theatre-going was far more of a threat to the moral behaviour and **salvation** of the people. The Church felt it was **sacrilegious** for men to dress up as women for the female parts in plays. As the plague was able to spread in the tight crowds of the theatre, the Church often claimed it was therefore God's punishment for such a pastime. When an earthquake occurred in 1580, an outbreak of plague the following year, and then a freak accident with some scaffolding outside a theatre, many were convinced that God was not pleased with the development of the theatre.

The Puritan Church felt that the theatre's teachings were **Popish** and could be dangerous by spreading Catholic ideas and thoughts at a time when Elizabeth I was making a new national Church based on the Protestant religion.

SOURCE A

Will not a filthy play, with the blast of a trumpet call 1000 to watch it, whilst an hours' tolling of the bell will call only 100 to church to hear the sermon?

A Puritan, John Stockwood, preaching in London, 1578.

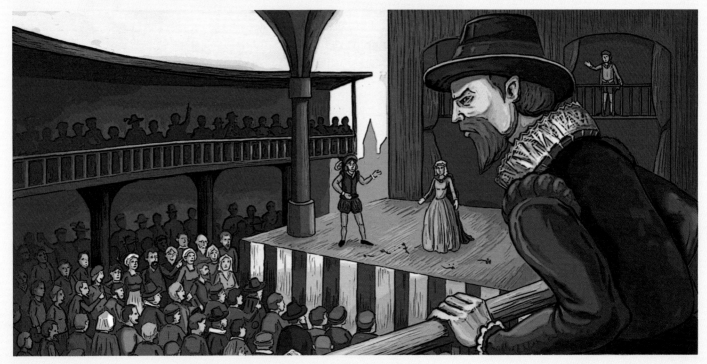

Plays are the invention of the devil, the offerings of Idolatry, the pomp of worldlings, the blossoms of vanity, the root of Apostacy, the food of iniquity, riot, and adultery: detest them.

Plays are masters of vice, teachers of wantonness, spurs to impurity, the Sons of idleness; so long as they live in this order, loathe them.

God is merciful: his wings are spread to receive you if you come betimes. God is just: his bow is bent and his arrow is drawn to send you a plague if you stay too long.

Stephen Gosson, a Puritan, in his book *The School of Abuse.*

Look upon the common plays in London and see the multitudes that flocketh to them. But I understand they are now forbidden because of the plague. I like the policy well if it hold still, for the cause of the plague is sin, and the cause of sin are plays. Therefore, the cause of plagues are plays.

A Puritan minister, objecting to theatres in 1578.

HISTORY DETECTIVE

Christopher Marlowe was another famous playwright of the time, who wrote plays such as *Doctor Faustus*. Unfortunately, he was allegedly killed during an argument by a dagger through his right eye. However, the only people who gave evidence were those who were with him during the argument. Investigate the mystery around his death, using the Internet and history books. Consider the following:

- Marlowe had spent time as a spy for the queen. Was this anything to do with his killing?
- Marlowe did not believe in God. He could be arrested and tortured for this and he may well have named names of others during this torture. Was this anything to do with his killing?
- Was Marlowe really murdered? Was his death another performance? Did he live on to write some of the plays that are said to be written by William Shakespeare?

ACTIVITY

Many of the people the Puritan Church were trying to reach in their preaching were unable to read or write. Imagine you are a Puritan and need to be able to explain to them why the Puritan Church felt that theatres and theatre-going were dangerous to their moral behaviour and the salvation of their soul. Design a poster that explains the issues the Puritan Church had with theatres. Think about:

- What you think about the popularity of the theatre. Where should those who are watching be in your view (as a Puritan)? (Source A)
- What does watching plays encourage? What might you learn from players? What will happen if you continue watching plays? What attitude should you have to plays and players? (Source B)
- What are the consequences of the theatre-goers' sin to all people, even those who do not visit the theatres? (Source C)

The Tragicall History of the Life and Death of *Doctor Faustus.*

Written by *Ch. Mar*

LONDON,
Printed for *Iohn Wright,* and are to be fold at his shop
Without Newgate, at the s . . . . . . he
Bi . 1636

The frontispiece of the 1610 edition of Doctor Faustus *by Christopher Marlowe.*

You have now completed this unit of work on Elizabethan society and in particular on poverty and changing attitudes towards it. You have also had practice answering questions that will help you prepare for your examination. Below is a typical example of an examination question.

Explain why many people were poor during Elizabeth I's reign.

[7 marks]

Examiner's tips

- Use the mark allocation as a guide to how many points you should make, how long you should take answering the question and roughly how long your answer should be.
- Be very clear before you begin to answer, what part of an event or change you are explaining – is it the long-term causes for example, or is it the immediate events.
- Do more than list key facts. Identify reasons and then explain or justify them.

Before you have a go at a question like this, read the simplified examiners' mark scheme, the student's answer and the examiner's comment.

Fact file

In your GCSE examination, you will be asked to explain why or how a significant event or change took place. It is a very factual question and requires you to know, understand and be able to apply historical fact and contextual information. It is far more than a description. It requires you to give the reasons for something, often in order to justify the event or change.

Simplified mark scheme

Level	Description of answer	Mark
Level 0	No answer or it does not answer the question	0
Level 1	General comments made. No specific contextual knowledge	1–2
Level 2	Identifies specific reasons but offers no explanation for them – similar to a description	2–4
Level 3	Identifies one specific reason and then explains it	4
Level 4	Identifies more than one specific reason and explains each of them, attempting to make links between them where appropriate 6 marks for one reason explained and another identified 7 marks for two reasons explained	6–7

Candidate's answer

There were lots of poor people because they could not support themselves and had no money. There were lots of reasons like inflation, bad harvests and the dissolution of the monasteries. The rise in population also caused people to be poor. Inflation meant that prices went up, especially the price of food during the four bad harvests in the 1590s. At the same time agricultural wages did not go up as fast. Enclosure of the farmland meant fewer jobs were available so employers could lower wages without much complaint. It became more difficult for people to afford the food that they needed.

Examiner's comment

The highlighted parts of the answer in blue show where the candidate has reached Level 1 as it is a very general comment on why people were poor.

The highlighted parts of the answer in red show where the candidate has reached Level 2. The candidate has identified a whole list of reasons why people were poor. These are historically correct but they do not explain any of them at this point in the answer.

Where the answer is highlighted in green, the answer becomes a Level 3. The candidates explains how inflation caused an increase in the number of poor.

To secure a Level 4 answer, the candidate must give an explanation for at least two contributory factors why people were the 'deserving poor'. The candidate could explain the long-term causes. This could include an explanation of the impact of the closure of the monasteries during the Reformation of Elizabeth I's father. This led to the removal of charity to tide people over until times were good again. The candidate could identify and explain a short-term cause of poverty such as heavy government taxation to pay for the expensive foreign wars of Elizabeth I. This was in a time when wages were low and so had a significant impact on the poor. A high-level answer would attempt to explain why people chose to be classed as 'idle poor' because living was relatively easy if they avoided being caught.

Now have a go at this question. Use the mark scheme and examiner's comment above to guide you.

Explain why attitudes towards the poor changed throughout the Elizabethan period.   **[7 marks]**

Chapter 4

Was England a great power during Elizabeth I's reign?

Before

The Portuguese and the Spanish had been colonising new territories in the Americas throughout the 16th century. Before the reign of Elizabeth I, little exploration had been done by the English. Newfoundland had been discovered during the reign of Henry VII in an attempt to find a route to the east by sailing north-west around America (the Northwest passage); and a new northern route to Russia (the Northeast passage) had been discovered during the reign of Mary I. The imbalance between the discoveries and colonisation in the new worlds by Portugal and Spain and that done by England worried Elizabeth I. She was afraid that England would become the poor relative – appearing weak and unable to benefit from trade with other countries. Not only that but she was worried that she would have to defend England from a Catholic alliance of France and Spain. She therefore needed to strengthen and enrich England with prizes from the unknown world.

Join the Navy

THE BALTIC

EUROPE

PORTUGAL

SPAIN

NORTH AMERICA

ATLANTIC OCEAN

WEST INDIES

AFRICA

THE SOUTH SEAS

SOUTH AMERICA

Good wages

Help spread Christianity

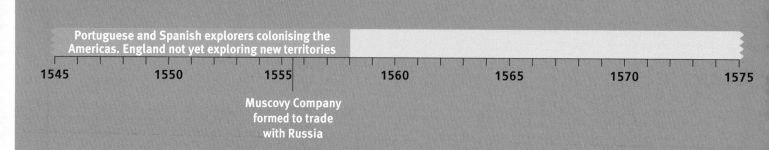

TIMELINE

Portuguese and Spanish explorers colonising the Americas. England not yet exploring new territories

1545   1550   1555   1560   1565   1570   1575

Muscovy Company formed to trade with Russia

After

Elizabethan voyages of discovery and exploration were highly successful in bringing back to England goods and treasure, whether discovered in the newly discovered lands or plundered from Spanish ships (privateering). English ships were also effective in battle, best illustrated by the battle of the Armada. After Elizabeth's death and with peace with Spain in 1604, the navy and its ships fell into decline. Also privateering fell out of fashion under James I who discouraged it. James I's son, Charles I, tried to revive privateering using Francis Drake as an example (see poster of 1626) with little success.

Colonisation of the Americas had been initiated by Sir Walter Raleigh in 1585 and 1587, however both attempts failed and it was not until 1607 that a permanent English colony was established in Jamestown, Virginia.

Poster printed in 1626. The heading reads: Sir Francis Drake Revived: calling upon this dull and effeminate age, to follow his noble steps for gold and silver.

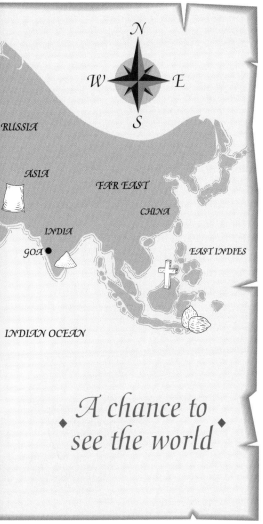

A chance to see the world

ACTIVITY

It is 1595 and you have signed up as a sailor on a voyage of exploration. You have heard much about these voyages and the dangers faced by the men on board. You know that if you are lucky enough to survive, you could be at sea for years. You need to explain to your wife why the voyage of exploration is so important and why you are willing to risk your life. Think about:

- How ordinary life in England will be better because of the voyages of discovery.
- How the economy of England could benefit because of the voyages of discovery.
- The spiritual and moral benefits of the voyages.
- The security of England.
- Your patriotic duty.

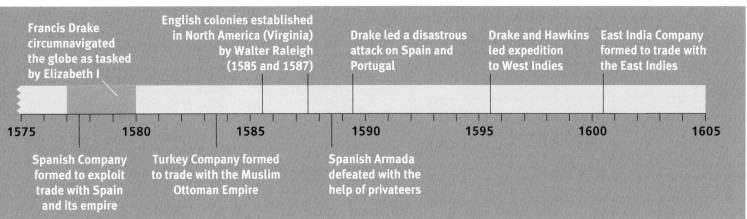

Francis Drake circumnavigated the globe as tasked by Elizabeth I

English colonies established in North America (Virginia) by Walter Raleigh (1585 and 1587)

Drake led a disastrous attack on Spain and Portugal

Drake and Hawkins led expedition to West Indies

East India Company formed to trade with the East Indies

| 1575 | 1580 | 1585 | 1590 | 1595 | 1600 | 1605 |

Spanish Company formed to exploit trade with Spain and its empire

Turkey Company formed to trade with the Muslim Ottoman Empire

Spanish Armada defeated with the help of privateers

4.1 How successful were the voyages of discovery of English sailors?

LEARNING OBJECTIVES

In this lesson you will:

- learn about the results of the voyages of discovery
- practise using source comprehension skills.

KEY WORDS

Exploration – *travels of discovery.*
Pioneering – *the first to discover a territory.*

Why did the English voyages of discovery take place?

With the Renaissance came new ideas in learning. This encouraged a spirit of curiosity and adventure. The reign of Elizabeth I was one of **exploration** and discovery. The voyages were mainly concerned with finding a route to Asia, travelling east from England and travelling west from England. The published reason for this burst of activity was to spread the Christian religion. In reality, such journeys were motivated by trade. Some explorers wanted to find short cuts to places they already traded with. Others wanted to expand the market for English goods, particularly in times of war when usual trade patterns were disrupted. Also the success of the Spanish, Portuguese, Italian and French explorers who had established vast new territories promised great hopes of new wealth and riches for all those who dared to explore the globe. England could not afford to be the poor relation surrounded by the growing wealth of these **pioneering** nations. She would become vulnerable to attack from her Catholic neighbours, particularly at a time when Elizabeth I was creating a new national religion that was not Catholic in nature.

SOURCE A

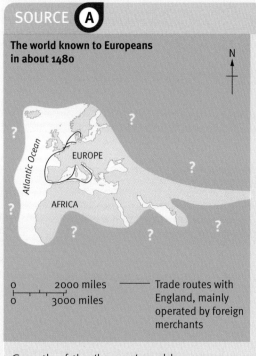

The world known to Europeans in about 1480

0 —— 2000 miles
0 —— 3000 miles
—— Trade routes with England, mainly operated by foreign merchants

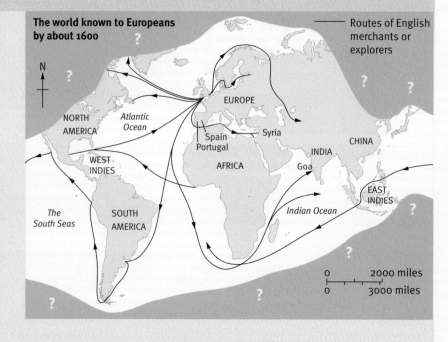

The world known to Europeans by about 1600

—— Routes of English merchants or explorers

0 —— 2000 miles
0 —— 3000 miles

Growth of the 'known' world.

Fact file

Trading companies were set up by royal charter in England to buy and sell goods in the new lands. The Turkey Company, for example, traded in spices and drugs from the Ottoman Empire while the East India Company traded in spices and silks from the Far East. In turn, they sold English goods, particularly woollen cloth, to the newly discovered lands. All voyages of discovery were funded by people who wanted a share of the profits. Elizabeth I herself sponsored many of the voyages and it is suggested that she made a 4000 per cent profit on one voyage alone.

SOURCE C

Being before this island, we espied two ships under sail, to the one of which we gave chase, and in the end boarded her with a ship-boat without resistance; which we found to be a good prize, and she yielded unto us good store of wine... Our General rifled these ships, and found in one of them a chest full of reals of plate, and good store of silks and linen cloth; and took the chest into his own ship, and good store of the silks and linen.

Francis Pretty, one of Francis Drake's gentlemen at arms, describing an event during their circumnavigation of the globe in 1577.

SOURCE B

... Here we gave ourselves a little refreshing, as by very ripe and sweet grapes, which the fruitfulness of the earth at that season of the year yielded us; and that season being with us the depth of winter, it may seem strange that those fruits were then there growing. But the reason thereof is this, because they being between the tropic and the equinoctial, the sun passeth twice in the year through their zenith over their heads, by means whereof they have two summers; and being so near the heat of the line they never lose the heat of the sun so much, but the fruits have their increase and continuance in the midst of winter. The island is wonderfully stored with goats and wild hens; and it hath salt also, without labour, save only that the people gather it into heaps; which continually in greater quantity is increased upon the sands by the flowing of the sea, and the receiving heat of the sun kerning the same...

Among other things we found here a kind of fruit called cocos... Within that shell, of the thickness of half-an-inch good, you shall have a kind of hard substance and very white, no less good and sweet than almonds; within that again, a certain clear liquor, which being drunk, you shall not only find it very delicate and sweet, but most comfortable and cordial.

Francis Pretty, one of Francis Drake's gentlemen at arms, describing the goods found in far-off lands during their circumnavigation of the globe in 1577.

ACTIVITIES

1. Look at Source A carefully. Describe the differences between the known worlds on the dates shown. Explain how this was of benefit to England – think about trade, culture, the spread of Christianity, colonisation.

2. According to Source B, what goods could explorers and sailors trade in and why were they not available in England?

3. Source C suggests that money was not just to be made on trading goods. How else could sailors on the voyages of discovery make their fortunes?

Cartagena, Colombia, 1586. The ship in the foreground may be Francis Drake's flagship, the Boraventure.

4.2 Case study: What dangers faced sailors like Francis Pretty on the voyages of discovery?

LEARNING OBJECTIVES

In this lesson you will:

- learn about the dangers faced by the sailors on the voyages of discovery
- develop empathy using source comprehension skills.

KEY WORDS

Mutiny – *when sailors turn against their master and try to take over command.*

Sacrifice – *an offering to a god to please them. It could sometimes be a human or an animal sacrifice.*

Scurvy – *a disease caused by lack of vitamin C.*

Tempest – *huge storm.*

What dangers did the sailors face?

During the voyages of discovery men could be at sea for months or even years. They suffered cramped conditions. Their food was salted to make it last but its quality was affected by poor storage and rat infestations. Diseases such as **scurvy** were always a threat. Discipline was harsh in order to make an example of anyone who committed an offence; such a large number of men in a small space for a long period of time had to be kept in order to prevent **mutiny**. In addition to all of these dangers, there were other more deadly ones faced on a daily basis.

The extracts in Source A are taken from the log of Francis Pretty, who was on board Francis Drake's ship on his circumnavigation of the globe, begun in 1577.

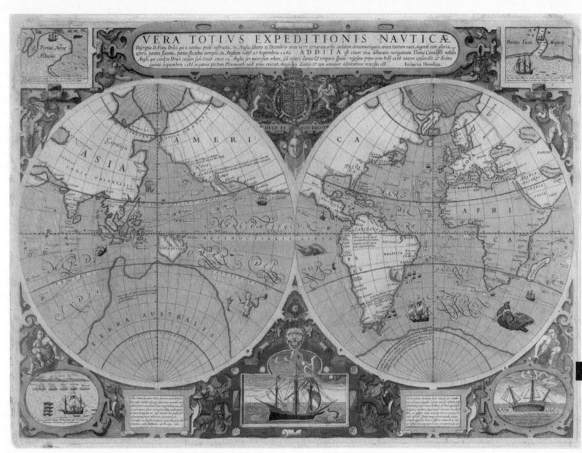

Francis Drake's circumnavigation of the globe by Jodocus Hondius, 1595.

The 15. day of November, in the year of our Lord 1577, Master Francis Drake, with a fleet of five ships and barks, and to the number of 164 men, gentlemen and sailors, departed from Plymouth, giving out his pretended voyage for Alexandria. But the wind falling contrary, he was forced the next morning to put into Falmouth Haven, in Cornwall, where such and so terrible a **tempest** took us, as few men have seen the like, and was indeed so vehement that all our ships were like to have gone to wrack. But it pleased God to preserve us from that extremity, and to afflict us only for that present with these two particulars: the mast of our Admiral, which was the Pelican, was cut overboard for the safeguard of the ship, and the Marigold was driven ashore, and somewhat bruised.

In this port our General began to enquire diligently of the actions of Master Thomas Doughty, and found them not to be such as he looked for, but tending rather of contention or mutiny, or some other disorder, whereby, without redress, the success of the voyage might greatly have been hazarded ...the place of execution made ready, he having embraced our General, and taken his leave of all the company, with prayers for the Queen's Majesty and our realm, in quiet sort laid his head to the block, where he ended his life. This being done, our General made divers speeches to the whole company, persuading us to unity, obedience, love, and regard of our voyage.

The 25. day of the same month... an island called Mogador... there came to the water's side some of the inhabitants of the country, shewing forth their flags of truce; which being seen of our General, he sent his ship's boat to the shore to know what they would. They being willing to come aboard, our men left there one man of our company for a pledge, and brought two of theirs aboard our ship; which by signs shewed our General that the next day they would bring some provision, as sheep, capons, and hens, and such like. Whereupon our General bestowed amongst them some linen cloth and shoes, and a javelin, which they very joyfully received, and departed for that time. The next morning they failed not to come again to the water's side. And our General again setting out our boat, one of our men leaping over-rashly ashore, and offering friendly to embrace them, they set violent hands on him, offering a dagger to his throat if he had made any resistance; and so laying him on a horse carried him away.

And being discovered at sea by the inhabitants of the country (Brazil), they made upon the coast great fires for a **sacrifice** (as we learned) to the devils; about which they use conjurations, making heaps of sand, and other ceremonies, that when any ship shall go about to stay upon their coast, not only sands may be gathered together in shoals in every place, but also that storms and tempests may arise, to the casting away of ships and men, whereof, as it is reported, there have been divers experiments.

The fifth of June, being in 43 degrees towards the pole Arctic, we found the air so cold, that our men being grievously pinched with the same, complained of the extremity thereof; and the further we went, the more cold increased upon us. Whereupon we thought it best for that time to seek the land.

From Francis Pretty's log 1577–1580.

ACTIVITY

Create a script for a conversation between Francis Pretty and Elizabeth I. Francis Pretty must outline all the dangers that the crew have faced on their journey. As he outlines each danger, Elizabeth I should respond by explaining why, despite the dangers sailors faced on the voyages of discovery, they must go ahead. Both Francis Pretty's and Elizabeth I's case should be very strong.

4.3 Francis Drake – a pirate or a great seaman?

LEARNING OBJECTIVES

In this lesson you will:

- assess the significance of Francis Drake
- practise cross-referencing sources.

KEY WORDS

Pirate – *seafarer who attacks any ship on the high seas, even those of their own country.*

Privateer – *seafarer who only attacks ships of 'enemy' countries.*

Modus operandi – *way of working.*

GETTING STARTED

Can you think of anyone who is considered to be both a hero and a villain at the same time? Robin Hood is a good example, but can you think of anyone else, perhaps someone alive today? How can there be such a difference of opinion about one person? Can the opinion of them change over time? Discuss your answers with a partner, then consider Francis Drake, who was considered both a **pirate** and a loyal, law-abiding servant of the queen at the same time.

Who was Francis Drake?

Francis Drake was born in Devon but his family moved to Kent during the religious upheavals of Queen Mary I's reign. At the age of 13, he became an apprentice on a small trading ship. When his master died, he left the ship to Drake. Drake sold this ship and returned to Devon to begin his seafaring adventures with his relative, John Hawkins.

Drake first became well known when he attacked the Spanish in the West Indies in 1567. He went on to circumnavigate the globe, an epic adventure which took three years. The new lands he discovered and the treasures he brought back with him resulted in him being knighted by Elizabeth I. He continually disrupted the movement of Spanish colonial trade. This played a vital role in English foreign policy by distracting the Spanish and their resources from an invasion of England. When the Spanish did eventually attack, Drake was a key figure in the defeat of the Armada.

SOURCE A

On April 13th 1579, about noon, two vessels entered port. No one knew who they were until a sailor cried out 'The English, the English!' I summoned, in King Philip's name, the few Spaniards who were about, but this had little effect because of the number of Englishmen who jumped ashore armed with guns, swords and shields. For three or four hours the Englishmen sacked the port. When I returned to the old church its vestments had been robbed. The picture that was on the altar was destroyed; the bell had been stolen. I learnt that the captain of the vessel was named Francis Drake.

A Spanish Roman Catholic priest, 1579.

SOURCE B

FRANCISCVS DRACO NOBILISSIMVS ANGLIAE EQVES, REI NAVTICAE AC BELLICAE PERITISSIMVS.

An engraving by Abraham Grimmer born in 1570 in Antwerp. It reads 'Francis Drake noblest English horsemen, king of the seas and specialist at warfare'.

Pirate or great seaman?

In his own lifetime and since, Drake has been regarded with mixed feelings. To some he was a national hero, a successful **privateer** and one of the most renowned seamen in all history. He discovered new lands, circumnavigated the globe, disrupted Spanish trading and even played a part in the defeat of the Spanish Armada.

To others he was an opportunist, portrayed as a bloodthirsty, money-grabbing, slave-trading pirate. In 1573, Drake joined with Tetu, a French pirate, to attack a mule train laden with gold and silver on the Isthmus of Panama. Although Tetu died, Drake and his men acquired significant treasure. As a result, the Spanish labelled him a vicious Protestant pirate and added his name to their list of most wanted men. Indeed, Elizabeth I used to refer to him as her 'pirate'. In his defence, Drake only plundered Spanish and Portuguese ships and usually did so with the quiet approval of his government. This **modus operandi** made Drake a privateer.

SOURCE

It seems evident that for the most part, Drake and other privateers were the unofficial agents of the crown. The Queen would disavow any complicity in the piracy efforts of Drake and others, but then would receive a portion of acquired bounty. This strategy was again employed in the raid of Cádiz, an Iberian port, in 1587. It was in England's best interest to disrupt the treasure route from the New World to Spain, because Spain used this revenue to fight the Dutch, an English ally. Drake's orders were left intentionally vague in his commission on March 15, 1587. He was not commanded to refrain from combat. This allowed the Queen the appearance of not sanctioning war.

Jeff Howell in Drake, Sir Francis: 'El Draque' The Dragon.

SOURCE

We should applaud Drake's care of the men who served under him. Their affection and respect was illustrated at Nombre de Dios in 1572, when, faced with the choice of seizing treasure, or attending to their wounded captain, they chose the latter. Furthermore, the vast majority of Drake's subordinate officers held him in the highest esteem. 'We all remain in great love with our general and in unity throughout the whole fleet.'

Susan Jackson of the Drake Exploration Society.

SOURCE

The accusation of profit seeking can only come from those who do not understand the principles and concepts underlying Elizabethan maritime expansion. All Drake's voyages were financed by joint-stock enterprise. This forced him to make a profit, in order to appease his backers; the biggest of whom was usually the crown. Modern-day, ill-informed critics, which include some professional historians, do not seem to appreciate how the vagaries of government policy often constrained and dictated Drake's actions.

Susan Jackson of the Drake Exploration Society.

SOURCE

Within three years of his second and final slaving voyage, Drake was harmoniously working with the escaped slaves in Panamá. He was the first white man to accord Blacks equal rights. This relationship was acknowledged by some of Drake's contemporaries. Hence, no acts of barbarity can be attached to Drake's name. For instance, when seizing ships off the west coast of South America, not one Spanish life was lost.

Susan Jackson of the Drake Exploration Society.

ACTIVITIES

1 Copy and complete the table using all the information in the unit.

	Evidence for	Evidence against
Drake was a slave trader, trading in people to make profit		
Drake had powerful backers that he had to please		
Drake was not backed by the queen		
Drake was a Protestant hero with no regard for the Catholic faith		

2 Was Drake a pirate or a privateer? Use the evidence you have collected to help you answer the question.

4.4 Get your sources sorted!

LEARNING OBJECTIVES

In this lesson you will:

- evaluate if Drake was a pirate or a privateer
- practise evaluating the historical context in which sources were produced.

KEY WORDS

Historical context – *what else was happening at the time; other significant events, changes, or opinions of the time.*

Infer – *suggest.*

Pirate or great seaman?

Drake began his circumnavigation of the globe in 1577. He set off with five ships and a crew of 164 men who thought they were going to the Mediterranean. Indeed, the voyage probably began as a planned raid on Spanish ships and ports. However, when he eventually reached America, Drake decided to continue the journey with just one ship, the *Pelican*. He renamed this the *Golden Hinde*.

During his journey, Drake and his men discovered it was possible to sail around the bottom of South America. He sailed further up the coast of the Americas than anyone had done. He plundered Chile and Peru and any Spanish boats he could chase on the way and filled his boat with spices, silver and treasure.

SOURCE A

Francis Drake at the River Plate, 11 December 1578 by Johannes Baptista, a Portuguese/Dutch engraver, 1610.

He found that Java was an island and was not connected to the southern continent.

On his return to England he was treated like a national hero. Elizabeth I boarded his ship and ate dinner with him. She then knighted him as Sir Francis Drake.

How do you evaluate the historical context of a source?

In your GCSE exam, you will be asked to examine why sources were published during an identified period. This will allow you to demonstrate a high-order analytical skill: evaluating the **historical context** of a source. You must examine the attribution of the source as well as understand the way the topic content has been interpreted by the author. This must then be set in its historical context using your own historical knowledge of the period. This question is usually awarded seven marks and is asked in the form of 'Why was this source published in...[date]?'

Answering an evaluation of a historical source question in practice

Why was Source A published in 1610?   **[7 marks]**

A low-level answer would simply describe what can be seen in the picture. A better answer would begin to look at the attribution of the source, describing when and by whom it was produced. A good answer would bring the above together. It would note that the source illustrates an incident in Drake's circumnavigation of the globe and was engraved approximately 30 years after. It would note that the engraver was Portuguese/Dutch and shows Francis Drake in a positive light which might not have been the case if the engraving had been done nearer the time of Drake's travels, as relations between Portugal and England were not good at that time. The answer might go on to outline the potential that Drake's findings would have for further exploration and trade and how receptive the people in the New World were to Drake's arrival. It would explain how popular opinion was divided at the time. Some saw Drake as a great explorer and others saw him as a pirate and at best a privateer. The highest-level answer would also discuss how Drake's travels were supported by Elizabeth I and how the success of his voyages and plunders were important in limiting the power of the Spanish in the New World.

TAKING IT FURTHER

Drake set off on his circumnavigation of the globe on a ship called the *Pelican* but returned on a ship called the *Golden Hinde*. Research what happened, when and why. You will find the answers you are looking for on the Internet, in an encyclopedia or a history textbook if you look up 'Drake', the 'Golden Hinde' or the 'Pelican'.

GradeStudio

Examiner's tips

- Use the mark allocation to guide you on the length of your answer, the number of points you should make and roughly how long you should spend on this answer.
- Look at or read the source carefully. You must understand the content and what it **infers** in order to establish the artist's/author's interpretation and viewpoint on the topic.
- Now look at the attribution of the source, the date of production and most importantly the intended audience. Ask:
  - When was it produced?
  - What else was happening at this particular moment in history?
  - Did this reflect popular opinion at the time?
  - Were they trying to influence anyone and why was this important at this time?
  - Why were they producing this evidence?

ACTIVITY

Follow this outline of what a good answer should look like and answer the question in full. Remember to refer to the examiner's tips.

A reconstruction of Sir Francis Drake's ship, the **Golden Hinde**. *It can be seen at Pickfords Wharf, London.*

4.5 What caused the Spanish Armada?

LEARNING OBJECTIVES

In this lesson you will:

- learn about how relations between England and Spain deteriorated so much that Spain attacked with the Armada
- practise using source comprehension skills.

KEY WORDS

Dutch rebellion – *the Dutch rebelled against the increasing control of Philip II of Spain in the Spanish Netherlands.*

Genoese loan – *money loaned by Italian bankers from Genoa to fund the Spanish army in the Netherlands to quell the Dutch rebellion. It was transported by ship.*

What went wrong with English–Spanish relations?

Spain was an old ally of England against France. Henry VIII had married Catherine of Aragon of Spain, the great aunt of Philip II. Philip II had married Elizabeth I's half sister, Mary I. When Mary I died, Philip II hoped that Elizabeth I would marry him. Yet, by 1558, the relationship between the two countries had changed beyond recognition; England and Spain were vicious enemies at war with each other.

Elizabeth I was always very concerned about the Netherlands for two reasons: it was an essential area for the cloth trade, which was England's main export; it was also a good place for enemies to launch an invasion on England and the Netherlands was part of the Spanish Empire.

Initially, Elizabeth I and Philip II of Spain were both worried about the threat from France so they were both keen that the Netherlands remain under Spanish control. However, Elizabeth I did not want Spain to increase its control in the Netherlands so encouraged self-government and the activities of English sea dogs such as Drake soured relations between Spain and England further. Elizabeth I's next move was crucial in the deterioration of Anglo–Spanish relations. She ordered the seizure of the **Genoese loan**. This was money loaned by Italian bankers to the Spanish army in the Netherlands to quell the **Dutch rebellion** against increasing Spanish control (the self-government Elizabeth I had encouraged). The Spanish were furious.

When the leader of the Dutch rebellion was assassinated, Elizabeth I felt she had to act before Spain defeated the rebels. Spain had signed an alliance with other Catholic nations and Elizabeth I became rightly concerned that they would join together and invade Protestant England. To take steps to avoid this happening, Elizabeth signed the Treaty of Nonsuch (see page 81) which enabled Elizabeth to send troops to the Netherlands as part of an agreement to give English protection of the country. Philip II became increasingly involved in plots to overthrow Elizabeth I from the throne of England.

SOURCE A

Peers, subjects and people of the kingdom (England), are freed from their oath (of loyalty to Elizabeth), and all manner of duty and obedience. They shall not dare to obey her, or any of her laws, directions or commands.

Papal Bull, 1570 – direction from the Pope in Rome directing all Catholics in response to the religious changes made by Elizabeth I.

SOURCE B

Francis Drake has returned from the Indies. He captured several of our towns and brought back 140 cannon, £1000 worth of pearls and £70,000 worth of gold and silver. Our ships should travel in groups. Even if they had to pay armed ships to guard them, it would be worth it.

Part of a report from a Spanish spy in England, 1586.

A servant of the Duke of Northumberland came to me and gave me the sign that his master and I agreed on. He said that his Lord and his friends in the north… would assure the Catholic religion and return to friendship and alliance with your Majesty.

8 October 1569. They have sent Northumberland's servant who spoke to me before, to say that they will… take possession of all the north country, restoring the Catholic religion. They ask only that they should be helped by your Majesty by a few soldiers.

Letters from the Spanish Ambassador to Philip II, September–October 1569, outlining his involvement in a plot to overthrow Elizabeth I and replace her with her Catholic cousin, Mary, Queen of Scots.

The Treaty of Nonsuch Signed at Nonsuch Palace, Surrey, England by Elizabeth I and Dutch Ambasssador 10 August, 1585

Terms of the treaty

- Elizabeth I to take the Netherlands under her protection
- Elizabeth I to send 6400 foot soldiers and 1000 cavalry
- Elizabeth I would pay £136,000 per year for the army's maintenance
- The Dutch to give the ports of Brielle and Vlissingen to England

The treaty of Nonsuch signalled the start of a war between England and Spain as it threatened Spanish interests in the Netherlands.

GradeStudio

Recall and select knowledge

The disruption of Spanish trade by the likes of Drake was the most important reason why relations between Spain and England deteriorated. Discuss whether you agree or disagree with this statement.

In order to do this to the best of your ability, complete the following steps which will lead you to a more comprehensive answer.

1 Copy and complete the following table on the causes of a deterioration of Anglo–Spanish relations. Use all the information you have learned about Elizabeth I's policies, actions and reactions to them and the information in the sources.

Cause of the deterioration of Anglo–Spanish relations	Questions to consider	Explanation of how this caused a decline in relations
Religious conflict	Elizabeth I's religious changes in England, the religious leagues forming around England	
Plots and conspiracies	Spanish involvement in plots to overthrow Elizabeth I	
The Dutch rebellion and Treaty of Nonsuch	Threat of an invasion from Europe Importance for English trade	
Trading rivalry	Disruption of Spanish trade International pride	

2 To write an answer to the question:

- Use the information above to explain how the acts of sailors like Drake contributed to a decline in Anglo–Spanish relations.
- Now identify and explain at least two other contributory factors.
- Make sure you conclude whether you agree or disagree with the statement in the question, or conclude another factor the most important, or conclude that it was a combination of contributory factors?

4.6 How was the English navy able to defeat the Spanish Armada?

LEARNING OBJECTIVES

In this lesson you will:

- learn about how the English navy was able to defeat the Armada
- practise using source comprehension skills.

KEY WORDS

Barrel staves – *lengths of wood joined together side by side to make a barrel.*

Crescent – *a half-moon shaped formation made by the Spanish ships. It makes it difficult to attack the centre because the ships on the outside edges close in to defend the centre.*

Naval base – *appointed port where supplies, ships, men and safety are available.*

The defeat of the Armada

The planned invasion of England by the Armada was delayed by a year. This was due to an incident known as the 'singeing of the beard of the King of Spain' where a significant portion of the Spanish navy was destroyed. In 1587 Drake sailed a fleet of ships into the port of Cadiz where Spanish ships were preparing for the invasion. Drake destroyed around 20 naval and merchant ships then continued to burn around 1600–1700 tons of **barrel staves** (enough to make 25,000 to 30,000 barrels in which to store food on a ship), and any other treated wood he could find along the Portuguese coast.

All seamen knew that food barrels had to be made of wood that had been treated to protect it from the weather, the wet and vermin. Ships also had to be built with treated wood to make them waterproof. The Spanish, determined not to delay the Armada for too long, quickly repaired ships and made food barrels with untreated wood which caused food to rot and ships to leak when the Armada eventually set sail in 1588.

The Armada was made up of 150 ships and 30,000 men. The plan was to sail to the Netherlands, join with another army of 30,000, land near Margate

SOURCE A

The new English warships were four times longer than they were wide. They were lower, faster and easier to steer.

The new English warships had improved heavy cannon to shoot at a longer range.

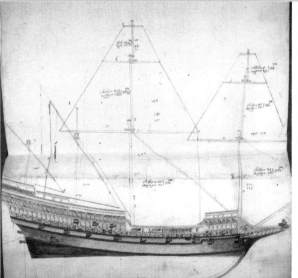

Spanish warships were two-and-a-half times longer than they were wide, which made them slow and difficult to steer. The Spanish also used four galleys, powered by oars and pulled by slaves, which could not cope with the Atlantic waves.

Spanish ships were designed to go alongside their enemy and board them.

Drawing of the new English warship by Hawkin's shipwright, Matthew Baker. By 1588, 25 of these were ready.

and take control of England. Philip II hoped that the mere presence of such a large enemy fleet near English shores would force Elizabeth I to make peace with Spain – but it didn't go according to plan!

Storm damage to some of the Spanish ships meant some were left at Lisbon. When they set sail again, the Armada formed a defensive **crescent**. Well armed galleons sailed on the wings, defending the slow-moving unarmed supply ships in the centre. They managed to keep this formation for a week. The English were unable to break it and the Spanish looked to be making good progress.

However, the wind and tide then forced the Spanish to anchor off Calais. The English saw their opportunity. Eight ships carrying tar, and with their guns loaded, were set on fire and sent towards the Spanish ships. The Spanish had expected the English to use this tactic to break the crescent and tried to move off, maintaining the formation, but the tide and the winds made this impossible. Instead, they scattered from their crescent formation and tried to sail north to escape the English fire boats. The English gave chase. Only 70 ships made it back to Spain. The rest were either destroyed by storm damage, met a gruesome end at the hands of the Scottish and Irish (where they tried to land), or were attacked by the English, who were in hot pursuit.

SOURCE B

*The campaign showed the vital importance of bases. The lack of a Spanish **naval base** near England was the basic reason why the Armada was unable to carry out its task.*

The English guns were neither powerful nor accurate enough to hit and smash a ship, except at close range. The Spanish cannon could do so, but their ships were not nimble enough nor the seamen skilful enough to bring their superior arms within close range of the enemy.

J. Fuller, *Decisive Battles of the Western World*, 1954.

SOURCE C

Armada victory medal – 'God blew and they were scattered'.

Grade Studio

Recall and select knowledge

Why did the Spanish Armada fail?

Before tackling the question read the sources and think about:
- the impact of the actions of Sir Francis Drake
- technology and the design of ships
- resources
- geography and wind patterns
- religious beliefs.

TAKING IT FURTHER

Elizabeth I used the defeat of the Armada in her propaganda campaign to convince the people of England that her decisions and directives were the right ones for their country. How would Elizabeth I have interpreted the reasons for the failure of the Armada to her own ends in her propaganda campaign?

SOURCE D

The geography and wind patterns of the English Channel played their part. The English Channel is shaped like a funnel. Once the Spanish fleet had entered the Channel, it became increasingly difficult to turn back if something went wrong. Secondly, the prevailing winds blow from the south west forcing the Spanish to the north east. In the naval fighting in the English Channel the English Navy with superior long-range gunnery, kept the Spanish from landing.

D. Murphy, *England 1485–1603*, 2005.

4.7 What contribution did the voyages of discovery and the defeat of the Spanish Armada make to the development of England?

LEARNING OBJECTIVES

In this lesson you will:

- learn about the contribution of English successes at sea to the development of England as a nation and world power
- practise cross-referencing sources.

GETTING STARTED

Look at a modern map of Europe. With a partner, look at the different countries. For as many as possible, describe some of the features of each country and the people who live there. How do you know so much about them? Have you or someone you know visited them or have you heard about them in the news? Would you recognise the people from a picture?

Look again at England. Why is it so important that England has a strong navy? Do you know of any recent military successes? How were they portrayed in the news and what benefit did they bring? Keep all this in mind as you analyse the impact of English success at sea during the Elizabethan period.

English success at sea during the Elizabethan period

English voyages of discovery and exploration not only expanded the known world, but opened that world up to English trade. This trade in English woollen goods with foreign spices, silks, foods and so on, brought great riches to the nation. The actions of the privateers also brought great profit to those who invested carefully, including Elizabeth I herself. England firmly established herself as a great trading nation.

The defeat of the Spanish Armada was celebrated as a sign from God that Elizabeth I was the rightful queen of England. A Protestant England had just defeated the most powerful Catholic nation had ever seen the world – so, God must be on Elizabeth's side. This victory also established England as a formidable naval power and ensured that England remained an independent country rather than being invaded by Spain and becoming a Spanish colony.

SOURCE A

Elizabeth I 'Armada portrait', unknown artist of British school, 1588. Elizabeth I and the defeat of the Spanish Armada. Through the windows can be seen the English navy and privateers beating the Spanish Armada. Elizabeth I's elaborate dress reflects the wealth of England. Her hand is resting on a globe strategically placed on the Americas where lands were being colonised and further defeats of the Spanish were taking place.

The defeat – mainly by sea and storms – of the Spanish Armada in 1558 solved nothing. There was still a successful Spanish army in the Netherlands, still Spanish support for French Catholics against the Huguenots, and still a risk of Spanish invasion: there were further armadas in 1596 and 1599.

C. Haigh, *Elizabeth I*, 1998.

What was the importance of all this for the future? Again, it would be too much to talk of the Elizabethan period as having undergone a 'commercial revolution'. Many of the major advances in trade and ship building... occurred after 1650 not before... Nevertheless, many future patterns had been set in motion during the Tudor period. One of the most important of these was the projection of English interest beyond Europe into a more maritime context. At this time there was still insufficient investment to make this as profitable as internal trade, but at least the process of diversification had been started.

S. Lee, *The Reign of Elizabeth I, 1588–1603*, 2007.

Queen Elizabeth I receiving Dutch ambassadors, 1573. As her power grew throughout Europe, foreign ambassadors met with Elizabeth I to negotiate trade deals and political alliances.

ACTIVITIES

1 Look at Sources A and B. They both refer to the impact of the defeat of the Spanish Armada on the development of England. How far do the sources agree about the impact?

    Think about:
    • wealth
    • power at home and abroad
    • religion
    • threat of further invasion.

2 Look at the attribution of both Sources A and B. Why might their interpretations of the impact of the defeat of the Spanish Armada on the development of England be so different?

3 Look at Sources C and D carefully. They both refer to the impact of the voyages of discovery and exploration on the development of England. How far do the sources agree about the impact?

    Think about:
    • wealth
    • trading patterns
    • power at home and abroad
    • threat of further invasion.

4 Look at the attribution of both Sources C and D. Why might their interpretations of the impact of the defeat of the Spanish Armada on the development of England be so different?

You have now completed this unit of work on whether England was a great power during Elizabeth I's reign. You have also had practice answering questions that will help you prepare for your examination. Below is a typical example of an examination question on this topic.

Which was more important to Elizabethan England: the voyages of exploration or the defeat of the Spanish Armada? Explain your answer. **[8 marks]**

Examiner's tips

- Use the mark allocation as a guide to how many points you should make, how long you should take answering the question and roughly how long your answer should be.
- Make sure that you are clear which two contributory factors or opposing views you are judging the strength of.
- Outline the case for one of the factors and then outline the case for the other. Take care, as the arguments you present will usually depend on who was asked and what their experience of the issue was.
- Conclude by judging which case is the strongest.

Before you have a go at a question like this, first read this simplified examiner mark scheme.

Fact file

In your GCSE examination, you will be asked to judge which is the strongest case for an argument. This is usually asked by giving a topic, then outlining two contributory factors or opposing viewpoints that you must first present a case for, and then judge which of these is the strongest. This is usually worth 8 marks.

Simplified mark scheme

Level	Description of answer	Mark
Level 1	General assertions that do not demonstrate knowledge of the period	1–2
Level 2	Identifies reasons why one is more important than the other and demonstrates some specific knowledge	2–4
Level 3	Explains the importance of one factor	3–4
Level 4	Explains the importance of one factor and then the other	5–6
Level 5	Explains why one factor is more important than the other factor	6–7
Level 6	Explains how the factors are interconnected	7–8

Secondly, look at the sample candidate answer below – noting the examiner's comment.

Candidate's answer

The voyages of discovery brought great wealth to England not only in the form of the new lands they discovered but also in the trading potential the new lands opened up. Trading companies such as the East India Company were set up to make trade with the new lands more direct by cutting out the middle man. The exploits of the adventurers such as Drake during their travels also brought great riches. Raids of ships were commonplace and often backed by the crown as such wealth was to be made.

The defeat of the Armada was also important as it showed England was a great sea power. It showed other European powers that England could mobilise sufficient ships at short notice by combining warships and merchant ships. The defeat of the Armada was a clear message to powerful Spain that they could not take whatever they wanted. The main aim of the Armada was to pave the way for an invasion of England so that Philip II of Spain could make England Catholic again. This was not the wish of the people of England and so its failure had great significance to the Protestant nation.

In conclusion, despite many voyages of exploration, the English privateers did not manage to dislodge the Spanish and Portuguese monopoly on colonies. They did give the country a sense of naval pride but their ultimate value was in the legends they created and their contribution to the defeat of the Armada. The defeat of the Armada by the merchant ships alongside the navy ensured England remained a strong Protestant independent country. It instilled a sense of national pride. It ensured that Elizabeth's religious reforms were now seen as blessed by God as they had defeated the most powerful Catholic nation in the known world. Elizabeth used the victory to raise her popularity with her public and had countless works of art and medals made to celebrate the success of her foreign policy. Her people, her parliament, and indeed kings of other nations now saw her as a formidable ally or enemy.

Examiner's comment

The parts of the answer highlighted in red show where the candidate has reached Level 4, as they explain the specific reasons why the voyages were important.
The parts of the answer highlighted in blue reach Level 5 as the candidate now explains why the defeat of the Armada was also important.
The last part of the answer highlighted in green certainly reaches Level 6. Having explained why both the voyages and the defeat of the Armada were important, the candidate goes on to point out why the defeat of the Armada was more significant.

Now have a go at the question below. Use the mark scheme and the examiner's comment above to guide you.

Which was more important to the defeat of the Armada: the merchant navy or the privateers? **[8 marks]**

ExamCafé

Welcome

You have now completed all the study units on Elizabethan England.

We now need to make sure that you prepare thoroughly for the examination so that you can apply this knowledge. Preparing for examinations is far more than reading your notes through again. Simply re-reading your notes and writing as much as you can on a topic in the exam will not secure you a high grade at GCSE. Working through the activities in this Exam Café section will help you to develop essential revision and examination techniques.

It will cover the most effective memory techniques while picking out the key facts on the topics that you'll need. It covers the best way to organise your time, your space and your notes. It highlights the difference between effective and ineffective revision. In preparation for the examination, it covers answering techniques for all styles of question, how to spend the first and last 10 minutes of the examination, and how to de-stress both before and during the examination.

Revision – getting organised

The difference between successful and unsuccessful revision strategies

Unsuccessful revision strategies

- Have trouble getting started and spend a lot of time getting the right equipment together rather than revising
- Simply read notes over and over again
- Do not prioritise revision but rather prioritise social life
- Revise with many distractions around
- Do not have a revision timetable and so put off the subject you do not like
- Start to panic and get stressed
- Revise too much or try to learn notes off by heart
- Do not start revising until the last minute

Successful revision strategies

- Have a revision timetable that is updated regularly. It spreads revision out over all topics including those which are not liked
- Use a variety of revision strategies that best suit own learning styles
- Have short sharp revision notes picking out the key words
- Some revision time is put aside for revising examination strategies
- Build time into revision for testing self on what have just learned
- Practise answering examination style questions under timed conditions creating plans for such answers the next day
- Keep a revision journal and note down any questions that arise during revision session so reminded to ask teacher

Organising your space

When you are preparing yourself for exams, think about the following:

- You will need a desk space as revising is more than just reading. Do not lie on your bed or work with a light behind you. Both will encourage you to feel tired.
- Have all your revision materials stored in a safe place so that you do not spend vital revision time looking for them.
- In the run up to the exams, drink less caffeine. It does not help you to absorb information and will prevent you getting much-needed sleep!
- Try to get more exercise and fresh air in the run up to exams, particularly if you are a learner who takes in more by doing.
- All your revision sessions should be timed and they must be objective-led. Decide what you are going to achieve at the start of the session and work towards that goal.

Organising your time

A revision timetable is essential. It helps you to spread out all your subjects and topics, making sure that you cover everything and give equal time to the subjects you like and those you do not like or struggle with. Look at the following timetable and the tips given around it. Try to create one yourself in this way.

At the end of each revision session take a break. During the break give yourself a treat. This could be a biscuit or a sweet. This helps motivate you to keep going, especially if you plan your rewards at the start of the session.

Revise in 40 min blocks. If you do solid revision during this time this is long enough to take in information but short enough to stop you becoming bored.

Recap time is essential. This is when you test yourself or get someone else to test you. If you do not do this, the information you have revised is likely to have been lost from your brain by the next day.

	40 mins	20 mins	40 mins	20 mins	40 mins	20 mins	10 mins
Mon	History	Break	French	Break	Science	Break	Recap
Tu_		Break		Break		Break	Recap
Wed		Break		Break		Break	Recap
Thur		Break		Break		Break	Recap
Fri		Break		Break		Break	Recap
Sat		Break		Break	Free time	Break	Recap
Sun	Free time	Break		Break		Break	Recap

Make sure you have a good spread of subjects throughout the week. Do not do more than three subjects per day/night. This will lead to confusion.

Perhaps laminate your blank revision timetable before you schedule your revision. You can then re-organise the sessions if you cover more or less in a session than you initially planned.

It is a really good idea to build in some free time. Revision is hard work but if you organise yourself properly and start in good time it does not have to take over your life completely.

Revision – what should I be revising and how do I do it?

Mnemonics

Using mnemonics is a really effective way to revise. Instead of learning pages and pages of information, you learn lists of key words in the form of codes. First you must highlight the key words you need to remember for a topic from your notes. Then pick out the first letter of each of these words. Rearrange the letters to either make a word or so that they stand for the first letters in a memorable phrase.

For example, when revising how Elizabeth I tried to win the loyalty of her people, a useful mnemonic could be:

Beth's **S**ecret **P**opularity **C**ampaign **M**anipulated **A**n **I**mage **C**risis

BSPCMAIC

B Ballads and hymns for the common folk
S Regular summer progress visiting nobles travelling through the countryside
P Prayers said by clergy to crowds for the salvation of God and the salvation of the queen
C Elizabeth I cultivated the common touch
M Elizabeth I presented herself as the mother of the people
A Annual celebrations to celebrate Accession Day
I Carefully controlled images
C Carefully staged charity by Elizabeth I

In the exam, write out your mnemonic to remind you of all the points that you need to make. Be sure to put a line through it immediately to show it is part of your planning and not your answer.

Key words and concepts

Read through your notes carefully. Use coloured highlighters to pick out the most important words and concepts. If you can, use a different colour to highlight different categories of information, like short-term and long-term causes or social, economic and political results. This will give you a visual reminder of the information when you recall it in the exam.

When revising about the Religious Settlement, the key words and concepts you would want to highlight are:

The Puritans generally were from the more educated sections of society such as lawyers and skilled workers. They were extreme Protestants who wanted all elements of the Catholic Church removed. They wanted a simpler, purer Church. Elizabeth I's compromise settlement which blended elements of the Protestant and Catholic Churches was not enough for them.

They did not act as one religious movement, rather they were divided into Moderates, Separatists and Presbyterians, based on their beliefs.

1. *Although not completely satisfied, the Moderates accepted Elizabeth I's changes and took positions in her new Church. They aimed to make small changes once they were in position, such as making priests wear simple robes.*
2. *The Presbyterians wanted to change Elizabeth I's Church but in particular wanted to remove the bishops and in place put councils of local, elected elders.*
3. *The Separatists were more extreme than both the Presbyterians and the Moderates.. They absolutely wanted to get rid of Elizabeth I's national Church, where each parish would decide its own direction. Their numbers were actually quite small.*

You can see how these ideas were totally opposed to Elizabeth I's idea of a uniform Church where bishops imposed her will.

Recording and listening to your revision notes

Listening to your own voice is a lot more effective than listening to someone else's. Actually reading out your notes is good revision preparation. Listening to them back over and over again can help the information go in subliminally. You could try to record the notes over some calming music to ease stress. Speaking your notes out loud as if you are teaching others also has the same effect.

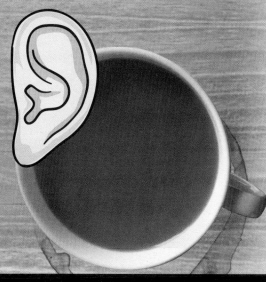

ExamCafé

Using sticky notes

These are a great way to revise. Write key words, concepts and ideas on them. Stick them in places you will visit often, such as the fridge door or the bathroom mirror. Looking at them every time you go there will increase the amount of time you revise and boost your memory. You can move the sticky notes around according to whether you know the information on them or not. You can encourage your family to test you using them too.

When revising the difficulties faced by Elizabeth I on her accession, some short sharp sticky notes to help you revise could be:

RELIGION
As father's marriage not recognised by Catholic Church neither was she as the rightful queen of England.

GENDER
Fought stereotypical images of women and their role, but also the question of marriage and succession was

MID-TUDOR CRISIS
Elizabeth I had a legacy of financial crisis, foreign wars, weak policies and religious persecution from the reigns of her siblings Edward VI and

WAR
On accession England was at war with France, a Catholic nation. Elizabeth I was worried they would launch an invasion through

Using index cards

Use index cards to record the main facts of the topic. Do not record detail on them. Start a new index card every time there is a development in the topic. Condensing the information and writing the cards out is only one part of the revision. Mixing them up and trying to put them back in the right order is a good way to practise processing the information. You could ask a friend to remove one of the cards and then you guess which one has gone. You could use them as prompt cards for question and answer sessions or keep them in your pocket to use as reference cards at the bus stop – but don't take them into the exam!

When revising how the treatment of the poor changed throughout the period, key facts on index cards could be:

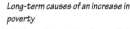

Long-term causes of an increase in poverty
Reformation and the closure of the monasteries
Inflation due to expensive wars
Growth in population

Short-term causes
1590's four bad harvests in a row
Wartime taxation
Woollen cloth, the main trade, came under competition from light foreign cloth

Ideas mapping

Turn the page landscape. You can filter more information this way through your peripheral vision. In the centre of the page, put the topic/subject you are revising. Coming out from the centre, have key ideas written along flowing lines. Make sure that these are brightly coloured as your brain is more receptive to colour. At the ends of these lines, put your ideas related to that information and then make connections on the diagram. Ideas maps work in the same way as your brain, by association and linking ideas together. Try to use as many pictures as possible. Many people are visual learners and this will tap into that part of your brain. Ideas maps are much easier to remember than pages of notes.

Known world expanded

Trading companies established all over the world

Expanded external trade of England

Increase in Elizabeth I's and England's power abroad

Foreign countries eager to create political alliances with England

Distracted the Spanish

Results

The rise of privateering and pirating

Increased wealth

New technology of ships developed

England remained independent Protestant country

Spain not able to dominate world politics any more

Confirmed Elizabeth I's position and her religious decisions

Results

Useful tool in Elizabeth I's propaganda campaign

English successes at sea

Voyages of discovery and exploration

Defeat of the Spanish Armada

Spread of Christianity

Causes

Promise of wealth

Age of exploration

Threat of becoming the poor neighbour to countries already colonising new lands

Promise of new territory to create an Empire

Activities of the 'sea dogs'

Causes

Dutch rebellion in the Spanish Netherlands. Perfect place for a Spanish invasion of England. Also important area for English cloth trade

Seizure of the Genoese loan by Elizabeth I

Spain's signing of Catholic Alliance with other Catholic nations

ExamCafé

Revision checklist

Look at the revision checklist below. Assess your knowledge and understanding of each of the topics listed before you begin your revision. The results will help you to create your revision timetable. When you have completed a session of revision, assess your knowledge again. You could also use this checklist to make sure you have revision notes on every topic.

Area	Details	I have little knowledge of this	I have some knowledge of this	I have a lot of knowledge of this
Was Elizabeth I Gloriana?	How difficult was the situation on Elizabeth I's accession? **Revision notes ✗ ✓**			
	What was Elizabeth I's concept of sovereignty and monarchy? **Revision notes ✗ ✓**			
	How successful was Elizabeth I in winning the loyalty of her people? **Revision notes ✗ ✓**			
	How far did Elizabeth I's image reflect reality? **Revision notes ✗ ✓**			
	Did Elizabeth I show weaknesses and misjudgements in the way she dealt with Mary, Queen of Scots and the Earl of Essex? **Revision notes ✗ ✓**			
What was the importance of religion in Elizabethan England?	Why did Elizabeth I regard religion as important? **Revision notes ✗ ✓**			
	How great a threat were the Puritans? **Revision notes ✗ ✓**			
	How great a threat were the Catholics? **Revision notes ✗ ✓**			
	How effective were Elizabeth I's policies towards these two groups? **Revision notes ✗ ✓**			

Area	Details	I have little knowledge of this	I have some knowledge of this	I have a lot of knowledge of this
	How effective were Elizabeth I's religious policies? **Revision notes** ✗ ✓			
Was Elizabethan society a divided society?	Why were poverty and vagabondage increasing? **Revision notes** ✗ ✓			
	Why was the government so concerned with poverty and vagabondage? **Revision notes** ✗ ✓			
	Why were the poor treated in the way they were? **Revision notes** ✗ ✓			
	Why was the Elizabethan period a great period for the theatre? **Revision notes** ✗ ✓			
	Why did different sections of society react towards plays and theatre-going in different ways? **Revision notes** ✗ ✓			
Was England a great power during Elizabeth I's reign?	How successful were the voyages of discovery of English sailors? **Revision notes** ✗ ✓			
	Was Drake a pirate or a great seaman? **Revision notes** ✗ ✓			
	How was the English navy able to defeat the Spanish Armada? **Revision notes** ✗ ✓			
	What contribution did English successes at sea make to the development of England? **Revision notes**			

ExamCafé

Exam preparation
Common mistakes

Often in exams we are tense and make some silly mistakes. If you are aware of the mistakes you could make before you go into the examination room, you will be better prepared and less likely to make them.

1 Often candidates do not look at the whole paper first. They open the paper and begin answering immediately. This is a bad mistake. If the question allows you to choose which questions you answer, you must make sure you look at them all first and judge which one you could answer best.

2 Often candidates do not plan their answers. They write down what they know in the order they think of this. If you have been asked to write a balanced answer to something, it is unlikely you will be able to do it in this way. Take a few minutes and, in pencil, write down the order you think you should mention things. When you have finished your quick plan, cross it out so the examiner does not think that is your answer.

3 A very common mistake is to misunderstand or ignore the command word in an exam question. This is the word that actually tells you what sort of answer the examiner wants, for example describe, explain, justify. Even if you write everything you know on a subject, if you do not do what the command word has asked, you will not get the marks. The most common command word not answered is 'explain'. For this, you must give the reasons for rather than just describing and listing.

4 Make sure that you use the mark scheme. The number of marks for each question is a really good guide to how much time you should and how many points you should make. Even if you write six pages, a question worth 5 marks can only be given a top mark of 5 so do not waste any more time on it. Equally, do not write a few lines for a question worth 9 marks.

5 Do not miss questions out. At least give them a try even if you're not confident, especially when there are sources there for you to use as references. The examiner will then be able to give you some marks. If you write nothing, you will get nothing.

What will the exam look like?

There are two sections to the paper:

Section A is your chosen Study in Development. This will either be Medicine Through Time or Crime and Punishment Through Time.

Section B will test the Study in Depth that you have just completed – Elizabethan England.

Section B questions are always set out in the same way so you can get an idea of what sort of questions are likely to crop up. Throughout this book, you have been developing the skills to tackle these sorts of questions. Look at the table on page 97 carefully. It sets out for you what style of question will appear in what part of the exam and also recaps the examiner's tips covered throughout the book. Make sure you are familiar with the information in this table. Understanding the style of questions is as important as understanding the topic information you have revised.

There is one compulsory source-based question, which is structured into three parts that can ask any of the following. This is worth 20 marks in total. Here are some examples of the type of question you may be asked.

a	According to the source why did… or what did… Use the source and your own knowledge to explain	• Use the language of the question in your answer. • Summarise what you think the source shows related to the question. • Use your knowledge and understanding of that historical era to explain the points shown or suggested in the source.
b	How far do the sources agree/disagree about…	• Study each source carefully, ensuring you understand what you read or see, inferences made and imagery used. • Read the question again to clarify the issue the examiner has identified as the focus of cross referencing. Do not simply write everything the sources agree on as it may be irrelevant. • Point out general themes, attitudes and tones the sources may agree on. • Give specific examples from the sources. • The question asks you 'how far' the sources agree so in order to make a judgement you must now give specific examples of how they may differ. • Now conclude and, in your own opinion, give your judgement. Use the language of the question in your answer.
c	Why was this source published in… Use the source and your own knowledge to explain	• Study the source carefully. You must understand the content and what it infers in order to establish the author's interpretation and viewpoint on the topic. • Now look at the attribution of the source, the date of production and, most importantly, the intended audience. • When was it produced? • What else was happening at this particular moment in history? • Did this reflect popular opinion at the time? • Was the author particularly high profile at the time? • Were they trying to influence anyone and why was this important at this time? • Why were they producing this evidence?
d	The source suggests that… Use the source and your own knowledge to explain how far you agree	• Make sure that you make reference to the source. • When a question asks you 'how far', it is provoking you to break the answer down into which parts you agree with and which parts you disagree with. • Often, if you look at the source from the experience of different people, it highlights those who would agree and those who would disagree. • Conclude how far you agree.

ExamCafé

You then have to choose one question from a choice of two. These are structured questions. Each question is structured into three parts and in total is worth 20 marks. Here are some examples of the type of question you may be asked.

a	Briefly describe… or What were…	• Each relevant point will be awarded with a mark so keep an eye on the mark scheme. • Give a good explanation for one or two of the points as this can be given a mark too. • Make sure that you make relevant points, not just simply list everything that you know.
b	Explain the arguments that were used for…	• Explain means to give reasons for. Do not simply describe, which means list. • Give explanations for at least two or three points in detail to secure the highest marks. • Keep referring to the question and its focus. Do not simply write everything you know on the subject.
c	How far did… or How successful was… Or which was more important. Explain your answer	• Read the question carefully to identify the actual issue you will be evaluating. Do not write everything you know about this topic. • Do not make generalised statements. Be clear with specific examples. • Perhaps begin with all the evidence for one case, then present evidence for the other. This helps you to ensure that you present a balanced view. • When you have presented both sides, you must conclude by making a judgement. It must overview the evidence you have based it on. • Do not save the best until last. No new evidence should be introduced in the conclusion. Without your reasoned judgement, you have not answered the question.

Finally

When you are in the examination use your time wisely.

Spend 20 per cent of your time reading through the questions, choosing which ones you can answer best and also planning your answers.

Spend another 70 per cent of your time actually writing your answers in full.

Finally, spend the remaining time (10 per cent) recapping. Read through your answers, checking you have written about all the points you made in your plans, ensuring that your answers flow and your spelling and grammar are good, and that you have answered the required number of questions.

Glossary

Accession – taking up the position of king or queen.

Admonitions – mild but earnest criticisms.

Allies – friends or countries who are joined for a common reason, usually to protect and defend each other and particularly in times when there is a threat of war.

Alms – charity, usually in the form of money.

Attribution – the writing, usually underneath the source, that describes who it was produced by, when, who the audience were, and sometimes why it was produced.

Barrel staves – lengths of wood joined together side by side to make a barrel.

Birth rate – number of births in a population.

Common field system – a system of dividing up the land in a parish for agricultural use begun in Anglo Saxon times.

Common land – land owned by one person but others have the right to graze livestock, collect berries for food or gather wood for fuel, etc.

Compromise – a settlement of a dispute in which two or more sides agree to accept less than they originally wanted.

Conformity – doing what is expected, in this case doing what is expected by Elizabeth I.

Crescent – a half-moon shaped formation made by the Spanish ships. It makes it difficult to attack the centre because the ships on the outside edges close in to defend the centre.

Death rate – number of deaths in a population.

Differentiate – show the differences between things.

Divine Right of Kings – the belief that the queen or king had been chosen by God to rule the country and therefore should not be disobeyed.

Douai missionaries – Jesuit priests. The University of Douai was founded by Philip II of Spain in 1426. Douai is in present-day France but it was once part of the Spanish Netherlands. It was where Jesuit priests trained.

Dutch rebellion – the Dutch rebelled against the increasing control of Philip II of Spain in the Spanish Netherlands.

Elite culture – what the rich did in their leisure time, such as hunting, fishing and reading/writing poetry.

Enclosure – hedges, walls or ditches used to enclose land into small fields and placed under private ownership.

Enlightened – embraced new ideas of the age, such as sharing responsibility for the poor rather than punishing them.

Erastian – somebody who believes that the state has authority over the Church in ecclesiastical matters.

Evaluate – judge.

Exploration – travels of discovery.

Favourites – those Elizabeth gave special attention and rewards to.

Genoese loan – money loaned by Italian bankers from Genoa to fund the Spanish army in the Netherlands to quell the Dutch rebellion. It was transported by ship.

Groundlings – those who paid a penny to stand and watch the play from the pit.

Historical context – what else was happening at the time; other significant events, changes, or opinions of the time.

House arrest – imprisoned but not in a prison. Putting Mary Stuart under house arrest meant that she could maintain full honour as a queen while being held captive.

Infer – suggest.

Inference – something that is suggested.

Inflation – an increase in the amount of currency being used but matched or outpaced by the unavailability of goods which leads to higher prices. Therefore, there is no benefit or real meaning to the rising level of wages.

Infrastructure – the basic organisation needed.

Interpretation – the meaning of something to someone; in particular, their view of an event.

Irresolution – lack of decision or purpose.

JP – Justice of Peace.

Jesuits – members of the 'Society of Jesus' founded by Ignatius Loyola in 1534. They were similar to monks but were able to travel to promote Catholicism.

Legislation – laws passed.

Licentiousness – pursuing desires aggressively and selfishly, unchecked by morality.

Line of succession – in line to the throne of England.

Loyalty – having a feeling of duty and devotion towards someone.

Marian exiles – Protestant priests who had been exiled during the Catholic reign of Queen Mary I.

Modus operandi – way of working.

Monopoly – total control, no competition on specified goods.

Mutiny – when sailors turn against their master and try to take over command.

National identity – a sense of what it is to belong to the country and be part of its characteristic features.

Naval base – appointed port where supplies, ships, men and safety are available.

Pioneering – the first to discover a territory.

Pirate – seafarer who attacks any ship on the high seas, even those of their own country.

Playwright – a writer of plays.

Popish – as the leader of the Catholic Church, the Pope, would like it.

Popular culture – what the general public did in their leisure time, such as bear-baiting and cock-fighting.

Poverty – the state of being poor.

Privateer – seafarer who only attacks ships of 'enemy' countries.

Privy Council – the committee that advises the queen.

Progresses – very public royal tours where the queen would travel to different parts of the country, greeting her people.

Protestant – a follower of a Christian movement separate from Roman Catholicism and the authority of the Pope.

Punitive – seen as punishments.

Puritans – Protestants who placed emphasis on preaching and wanted plain churches and no ceremonies.

Renaissance – a rebirth or revival of, for example, culture, skills or learning, that had been forgotten or previously ignored. Began in Italy in the 15th century.

Sacrifice – an offering to a god to please them. It could sometimes be a human or an animal sacrifice.

Sacrilegious – against the will of God.

Salvation – saving of the soul.

Scurvy – a disease caused by lack of vitamin C.

Self-interest – main concern is the promotion of oneself.

Sovereignty – supremacy as ruler.

Spanish Armada – the Spanish fleet of ships went to overthrow Protestant rule in England.

Stability – consistency, things remaining the same for some time giving the opportunity for them to settle.

Stereotypes – deeply entrenched ideas.

Surplice – the white tunic usually worn by Catholic clergy.

Tempest – huge storm.

Treason – acting unlawfully against your country and your monarch.

Vagabond – an idle poor person, also known as a sturdy beggar.

Vagrant – sturdy beggar, idle poor.

Index